MILLION DOLLAR SEED

How Unusual Acts of Faith Produced
Million Dollar Results

Pastor Allen Brown

BUILD OUR KINGDOM PUBLISHING
BUILD OUR KINGDOM.COM
PO Box 1079, Stroudsburg PA 18360

Million Dollar Seed

Copyright © 2020 by Build Our Kingdom Publishing, LLC and Allen Brown
Published by Build Our Kingdom Publishing, LLC

All rights reserved. This book or any portion thereof may not be reproduced or used in any manner whatsoever without the express written permission of the publisher except for the use of brief quotations in a book review.

Printed in the United States of America

1st Edition May 2020 First Printing

ISBN for paperback: 978-1-7350588-0-1

ISBN for Ebook: 978-1-7350588-1-8

Build Our Kingdom Publishing, LLC. PO BOX 1079, Stroudsburg, PA 18360

www.BuildOurKingdom.com

Edited by: Angela Ivey ~ Amos Ogechi

Scripture taken from the New King James Version®. Copyright © 1982 by Thomas Nelson. Used by permission. All rights reserved.

Scripture quotations marked (NIV) are taken from the Holy Bible, New International Version®, NIV®. Copyright © 1973, 19 78, 1984, 2011 by Biblica, Inc.™ Used by permission of Zondervan. All rights reserved worldwide. www.zondervan.com The "NIV" and "New International Version" are trademarks registered in the United States Patent and Trademark Office by Biblica, Inc™

Although the publisher and the author have made every effort to ensure that the information in this book was correct at press time and while this publication is designed to provide accurate information in regard to the subject matter covered, the publisher and the author assume no responsibility for errors, inaccuracies, omissions, or any other inconsistencies herein and hereby disclaim any liability to any party for any loss, damage, or disruption caused by errors or omissions, whether such errors or omissions result from negligence, accident, or any other cause.

This publication is meant as a source of valuable information for the reader, however, it is not meant as a substitute for direct expert assistance. If such level of assistance is required, the services of a competent professional should be sought.

Table of Contents

Dedication i

Acknowledgment iii

Introduction: What Is The Million Dollar Seed? 1

P H A S E O N E: Life Before Jesus Christ 4

    Chapter 1: Life Before My Relationship With Jesus Christ 5

    Chapter 2: I Think I Am An Entrepreneur 19

    Chapter 3: Hustle To Hustle 29

    Chapter 4: I Am Never Getting Married 41

    Chapter 5: I Once Was Blind Now I Can See 53

P H A S E T W O: Life Knowing Jesus Christ 59

    Chapter 6: Hearing God's Voice For The First Time 61

    Chapter 7: Learning To Trust God's Timing 69

    Chapter 8: Yes, I Am Saved! 79

    Chapter 9: Get Out Of Your Comfort Zone 85

P H A S E T H R E E: Life Trusting Jesus Christ 93

    Chapter 10: God Are You Serious? 95

    Chapter 11: Listening To God's Detailed Instructions 103

    Chapter 12: Before I Formed Thee, I Have Ordained Thee 111

    Chapter 13: God Showed Me A Sign 121

    Chapter 14: Eating Out Of God's Hand! 131

    Chapter 15: The Promise 145

Chapter 16: Exceedingly More 159

Chapter 17: Only God Knew! 175

Chapter 18: Tell The World 191

Conclusion: Understanding The Seed **199**

Message From The Author's Wife **205**

About The Author **205**

About Build Our Kingdom Publishing **209**

DEDICATION

To my Lord and Savior, Jesus Christ, for blessing me with everything in life!
To my wife, Melissa, whom God has given me to make me a better man. I love you for all that you have done. To my soldiers, Elijah, Isaiah, Josiah, and Micaiah: My four sons that God has blessed the world with. I love you all!
To my parents, Elijah and Carolyn Brown, for raising me and guiding me to be the man I have become. Forever grateful for your love and support.

ACKNOWLEDGMENT

To all my family and friends who have been a part of my journey; I want to give you all special thanks.

My Aunt, Nell, who gave me my first professional clipper when I was fourteen years old; my sister, Carol who, in 1996, bought me my first personal Bible. It was the first bible where I read the entire Gospel of Matthew. My brother, Todd, who had no choice but to be my punching bag and my first client as a barber.

The late Bishop Lester Williams, my first pastor. I'm forever grateful that God used you as my entryway into the Kingdom; Bishop Horace White, for being my spiritual covering and supporter; Bishop Shirley G Williams, my first Momma in the Gospel; Bishop Eva Stinson Givens, for always giving a word of encouragement. My boy, Gregory Beauvais, for always being there on time to pass me key information to push me forward. My boy, Rockwilder, my God-Given spiritual brother who is also the best music producer on the planet.

INTRODUCTION

WHAT IS THE

MILLION DOLLAR SEED?

Before I share how God blessed me with divine connections, a business that generated millions, and additional income opportunities, I think it would be especially important for me to explain to you what this book is **not**.

The *Million Dollar Seed* is not a book that lays out how you will make a million dollars tomorrow or even become rich due to some kind of scheme presented in the pages herein. It's not a book filled with fake promises to give you false hope about your future and the success you can have. What you will find in the pages of this book are my personal acts of faith and my trust in the Lord that allowed me to receive million-dollar results.

I believe what I went through to be greatly blessed by God required a lot of faith. I say this because every time I tell people my testimony, they say, "Wow, that must have taken a lot of faith!" While I do know that I exercised a lot of faith when I finally received what I was believing God for, the journey to obtain it was not that bad. It did require trust in the lord, a lot of patience, managing my frustrations, constantly seeking God, and ultimately being obedient to the instructions God gave me.

I remember thinking before I prayed to God about my situation, *Could God really bless me?* I believe it was the spirit of doubt trying to come in. However, what I discovered in my journey was that, as long as I kept moving forward, God kept giving me the next step, pushing toward the blessing. It's important that when God speaks to you and gives you direction, you take the next step.

FAITH JOURNEY WITH THE LORD

One of the greatest stories of faith in the bible is that of Abraham. **Genesis Chapter 24:1** reveals that God blessed Abraham in all things. **"Now Abraham was old, well advanced in age; and the LORD had blessed Abraham in all things." Genesis 24:1 NKJV** Abraham received the blessings of the Lord as a direct result of his obedience and faith in God. He was not perfect, and it's documented that he had many struggles along the way. However, the key thing is that he stepped out on faith, started his journey, and received the promise from the Lord.

The million-dollar seed story is about my life and the journey I took after I heard the Lord respond to me in prayer. I wanted my life to change because I was tired of working every day and not having the time to be with my family. I made my request known to God and received specific instructions that I lay out in this book. Unlike Abraham, who started his journey right away, I was somewhat hesitant at first. After failing horribly from my disobedience, I then turned back to God and started doing everything He told me to do. Even when it didn't make sense to me, I moved forward. The result was unexpected blessings that exceeded my expectations.

MY JOURNEY WITH THE LORD

I'm humble enough to say that in no way do I compare myself with Abraham, but I can identify with him because of the acts of faith I took once I heard the Lord speak to me. My journey presented some challenges, and like Abraham, I acted out of doubt a few times. Nevertheless, I never stopped moving forward after believing what God told me.

I want to share with you how my life changed once I decided to take my journey with the Lord Jesus Christ. I like to look at my life in three phases. Life before I knew Jesus Christ, Life knowing Jesus Christ, and my Life *trusting* Jesus Christ. Each phase has its importance in my development in God. I believe each phase of my life prepared me for the next.

Hopefully, you'll get a lot from this book as each chapter sets the stage for how it all turns out in the end. As you flip the pages and begin reading, don't read with the mindset to "just read." Read to learn from my decision to obey God, my experiences, my faults, my struggles, and the wisdom God gave me to make good decisions that have changed my life forever. Trust me, you can gain a new perspective that can also change your life forever.

Let's Begin!

PHASE ONE

Life Before Jesus Christ

CHAPTER 1

LIFE BEFORE MY RELATIONSHIP WITH JESUS CHRIST

I really didn't understand why God would tell me to start giving all my money away. Why would that make any sense? It was extremely puzzling--up until I gave away my last $17,600 to a complete stranger. It was at that moment that it all made sense.

Millions in sales! Who would've ever thought by applying total faith in God and trusting His leading, it would bring successful businesses and spark ideas that generated millions of dollars? Honestly, I had my doubts at times, but when I finally stepped out in total faith and trusted the Lord to bless me, He did it in ways I would have never imagined.

My main prayer was for God to give me time to be with my family. I could no longer take the demand for the long hours I was spending in my barbershop. Yes, I was the owner, but because I was an owner-operator, it was no different than having a 9 to 5 that puts a demand on me to be there all the time, including the weekends. Maybe you can see why I prayed to God for a change.

GOD DID THE UNTHINKABLE

What happened approximately three and a half years after that prayer boggles my mind every time I think about it. I am sometimes still in shock, thinking about what God did in my life to open major doors for success. I can't believe how He took my actions in faith and blessed me beyond what I could have possibly dreamed. He does promise in His Word to do exceedingly, abundantly above what we ask or think. **"Now to Him who is able to do exceedingly abundantly above all that we ask or think, according to the power that works in us," Ephesians 3:20 NKJV** Sometimes we read this scripture, but it's not until God does it for you that it completely blows your mind. I want to share with you how my life has been changed, as well as help you to believe that God can exceedingly and abundantly bless your life.

WHERE THE JOURNEY BEGAN

I know 100% that Jesus Christ was in my life before I came to truly know Him in the earthly realm. I also know He has called me and given me tasks and assignments to carry out on the earth for His sake! Knowing how He has allowed me to be successful and a blessing to the body of Christ explains a lot about why I had to go through what I went through. Why I had to be born where I was born and have the parents that I had. The struggles, challenges, and the ups and downs throughout the journey were all ingredients ordained by God to create the story you are about to read. My story. My testimony. It's the reason why I must start from my childhood so you can see how God is extremely intentional from the time you are born to the time you connect with Him, and even unto death. I greatly encourage you to allow the Holy Spirit to speak to you as you read through each chapter. I'm hoping that you will grow in understanding and wisdom from each point I'll share with you, as well as build a stronger relationship with our Lord Jesus Christ.

ALLEN BROWN ENTERS THE EARTH REALM

I started off with very humble beginnings. I was born in 1974 to Elijah and Carolyn Brown in Brooklyn, New York. I lived with my parents in Flatbush, Brooklyn with my other two siblings--Carol, my older sister, and my younger brother Todd. My memories from my first four years are a little bit sketchy, but I remember that my parents put in a lot of work to raise us up. My father was a New York City bus driver, and he was exceptionally good at many of the things he did. My mother was equally as hardworking, making sure all was well with us at home, and that we were raised to be the kind of adults we are today.

BORN IN BROOKLYN BUT QUEENS RAISED ME

In 1979, we moved to Queens, New York. I remember celebrating my fifth birthday in our modest three-bedroom middle-class home, surrounded by family and friends. My earliest memory of Queens centers around how diverse the community was. I grew up around all types of cultures. I had German friends, Indian friends, Asian friends, black friends, white friends, etc. As I visited my friends' homes, I was exposed to a variety of cultures, even from a young age. The biggest blessing from that experience is it gave me exposure to all kinds of people. I believe it's the reason why I don't have many racial hang-ups so many people struggle with today. It was a community of love and support. Although there was a little racism around, Queens was still a good place to grow up, and I thank God that He placed me there so young.

I can share a lot about my life from ages six to eleven growing up in Queens, but age eleven is when I really started my journey. That's when I started learning about business and getting out on my own.

SHOW ME THE MONEY!

I became very ambitious. I was the type of kid who was always looking for ways to make money. The first business I can remember having was cutting grass in my neighborhood. I like to call it my landscaping business. I would ask my father if I could use his lawnmower to cut grass for people to make money. This was basically my first experience in the art of negotiation because my father would always say, "If you cut our front and back yard first, then you can use my lawnmower." These little negotiations taught me that if I wanted to achieve my goals, I would have to find ways to make others release their own resources for my use.

> *"Wisdom is the principal thing; Therefore get wisdom. And in all your getting, get understanding."* **Proverbs 4:7** You will notice the **wisdom and understanding notes** added along the way to offer you more insight as you read. I will be sharing some of the wisdom – both the wisdom that was developing and the wisdom I applied at different stages in my life.

> **Wisdom and Understanding Note**
>
> Many people have the tools you need to succeed. Even when you don't have the money to finance the tools, look at what you can do for others so you can, in turn, use what they have to benefit your purpose.

I'd typically take my brother with me because he was developing a mindset like mine. We would go from house to house and knock on doors, asking if we could mow their lawns for money. This was the early-mid 80's, so we would usually charge $5 for the front and around $7 for the backyards. Every Saturday, we'd go out as soon as we were done mowing our own lawn, and we wouldn't come back until we had made around $100. That was the way it went all spring and summer.

As I mentioned earlier, I was always looking for ways to make money, so when winter came, I saw another opportunity to make some cash. I would repeat the same negotiation with my father, and after shoveling the snow at our house, I would take his shovel and go with my brother to help other people shovel their snow, at around the same price we charged for mowing lawns. We would split this money between us, and from this, we started learning independence. I went on to start buying things for myself from my savings at that very age.

> **Wisdom and Understanding Note**
>
> I learned from going door to door that getting a "yes" was a number's game. My brother and I would knock on many doors before we got someone to say "Yes, you can cut the grass or shovel the snow." It was like knocking on 100 doors to get 10 people to say "yes." If you think about the numbers, you can pretty much get an idea of how much work you have to put in to get your desired income results.

As I continued to grow in the mindset of doing my own thing, I started to pay more attention to how money was made and how to get it on my own. I remember walking out of Grand Union grocery store in Queens with my mother. It was located at the Franhill strip mall, not too far from where we lived. As we left the store, two young boys asked my mother if they could help her put the grocery bags in her car. I can't remember if she let them help her or not, but I watched them help someone else and saw the person give them money for carrying their grocery bags to their car. The very next day, I went to Key Food, which was another local grocery store, to try my hand at the same service. As people came out of the store, I would simply ask, "Do you need help carrying your bags to your car?" This would get me a lot of change--sometimes $5 or $10--every time I would go there.

> **Wisdom and Understanding Note**
>
> Always pay attention to how others are making money. What they are doing in one area, you may be able to introduce in another area.

SELLING STUFF YOU CAN GET FOR FREE

When I was in the seventh grade, I had another hustle. My good friend, Marlon, had two younger sisters, Bridgett and Raquel, who had received an autographed photo from a group called Audio Two. They were so excited about the autograph when they were showing it to me. I asked them how they received it, and they told me that they had joined the Audio Two fan club and that the group had sent the autographs to them. The next day at school, I started marketing these autographs to students--basically all the girls. I told them that I had a cousin who was a road manager for LL Cool J, Kool Moe Dee, and all the hot music artists at that time. I then charged $5 to $10 for an autograph from their favorite music artist. Basically, I made a list of the autographs they wanted and sent the request to the appropriate fan club. When I got the autographs in the mail, I sold them to my "customers." Although I didn't make a lot of money doing this, I still had that hustler mindset that made me keep trying to get something out of nothing.

> **Wisdom and Understanding Note**
>
> Opportunities are all around us to make money. Many businesses started by simply providing a service that does the

> things people don't want to do or don't know how to do. I know that I have paid for services that, had I done a little research, I could have done myself and saved money.

I WANT A MILLION DOLLARS!

When I was about thirteen or fourteen, I would sit and think about ways to get one dollar from a million different people. I didn't know how to go about it, but I knew that if I could achieve it, it would make me a millionaire. Little did I know it was the beginning of a millionaire's mindset. Looking back, I realize it was particularly important that I meditated on such things.

When I turned thirteen, my friend Jonathan started cutting hair, and my brother and I started letting him cut our hair. Since we were gradually becoming independent, we didn't want to go with our dad to his barbershop. Dad didn't really care about the hairstyles we wanted; he just told the barber to cut all the hair off. Since we were tired of this, we had Jonathan cut us the styles we wanted. Sometimes, we paid Jonathan from the little money we had saved up. Other times, he did it for free. Later, Jonathan left the neighborhood to attend barber school and started cutting hair in Harlem, New York. After that, there was a void in the neighborhood for a barber. Thinking about how he had cut my hair, I became inspired to start cutting hair myself. I took some of the money I had saved up from my lawn mowing and snow shoveling and bought myself a clipper--not the professional type used by professional barbers. This was a cheap clipper that you can buy in any drug store.

> **Wisdom and Understanding Note**
>
> So many people never get started on their dreams because they feel they need the best tools or equipment to get started. With that way of thinking, you may never get started. My skills were greatly enhanced using that cheap clipper.

I started practicing my barbering skills on my little brother and myself. Initially, I was shooting for a "bowl cut," but just ended up messing his hair up. I must have used two amateur clippers before I got my first professional ones.

I had gone with my mother to Aunt Nell's beauty salon to get her hair done. There, I spotted a pair of Andis liner clippers lying unused in her office. I remembered going to the barbershop with my dad and seeing the barber there with the same clippers. I asked Aunt Nell for the clipper, but she said I couldn't have it. The truth is I didn't even know where I could buy that clipper. I didn't even know how much it cost.

It wasn't long after the first visit that I went with my mother again to Aunt Nell's beauty salon. When I walked in her office, that same clipper was there in the same spot. I asked her again if I could have it, and she told me "no" again. This time, I asked her where I could buy an Andis clipper. She told me that a guy came around and sold them. That day, I left thinking I had to get myself one soon. I wanted my shape ups to be sharp, and the cheap clipper I had was not allowing me to do that.

It was about time for my mother to get her hair done again. I went along, specifically to bug Aunt Nell for the clipper. As soon as I walked into her salon, I went straight to her office only to see the clipper sitting in the same exact spot. I said to her, "Aunt Nell, that clipper is in the same exact spot as before. Do you even use it? Can I please have it?" She turned to me and said, "Go ahead, Allen. You can have the clipper." That's how my aunt became the person whom I received my first professional clipper from. After I got this clipper, I started learning how to use it. As I got better, I started cutting the hair of kids around the neighborhood to make money.

Wisdom and Understanding Note

Even though I didn't know what to call this character trait at the time, I later discovered it was called being persistent. When you are determined to acquire something or achieve something, you can't let "no" stop you. Now, I understand I may have been a pest in bugging Aunt Nell, but my persistence paid off. Thanks, *AUNT NELL!*

FLIPPING BURGERS TO MAKE MONEY

Later, my childhood best friend, Michael Simpson, started working at Burger King. He was sixteen at the time. I asked him if he thought they would give me a job working there even though I was only fourteen at the time. He spoke to the manager who said "yes." I was surprised because they let me work without getting my working papers, and they gave me hours after the legal time limits for a fourteen-year-old. I worked from five to closing, which was midnight. At first, I thought this was going to be the coolest thing ever. This was my first job with an hourly wage, and I was super excited. I was just thinking of all the sneakers and clothes I was going to buy on Jamaica Ave. The "Ave," as many called it, was the place where many people in Jamaica Queens, New York, shopped. I worked there for about three weeks before they gave me my first paycheck for the first two weeks of working. I will never forget the day I received that paycheck.

The manager handed me an envelope with my name on it. I sat in the dining area by myself to open it up. All I can remember saying to myself was *What the hell is this?* After a bunch of deductions, I had only made $94 for two weeks' worth of work. I quit that job the very next day. I took my paycheck and bought myself an Oster professional clipper for about $90 at the Long Island Cutlery in Queens. To date, that was the last and only hourly wage job I've had in my life.

Wisdom and Understanding Note

Something I realized early in life was that hourly wages were not going to make me rich. I don't knock those who prefer working for hourly wages, but the truth is it puts a cap on what your full income potential can be. It is important to focus on making each one of your hours produce future income. Most of the world's population has not been taught to earn outside of an hourly wage.

Now that I had more tools to cut hair with, I asked my parents if I could set up a barbershop in the basement of my home. They agreed, and I started cutting hair for more of the neighborhood kids in my basement. I used some milk crates, an overhead shop light, and an old mirror from my grandmother's house, and set it up in the corner of the basement. I also hooked up an old stereo system I had for the music. I was charging $5 for each haircut and growing in my skills.

> ### Wisdom and Understanding Note
>
> LOL! The Basement Barbershop. I remember those days! It's funny to me now because I didn't consider this to be my first barbershop. It was just a place I had set up shop using milk crates and used furniture, charging $5 for haircuts. I know in some areas, this would now be illegal without the proper permits and licenses. However, the wisdom in that move is to just get started by any means necessary.

Around this time, I must have inspired my friend, Marlon, to cut hair. Marlon moved a little bit faster than me in learning the trade after he met this guy named Sam. Sam, who also was a barber, basically introduced Marlon to a barbershop in Jamaica Queens, where he learned barbering in a short amount of time. I didn't see Marlon in the neighborhood for about four months, but I had heard he was getting very good at cutting hair. When I finally caught up with him, I asked him if he thought I could get a chair in the barbershop. Marlon said, "Don't worry, I'll talk to Marty on your behalf." Marty was the Latino guy who owned the shop. Marlon told me this three different times, but when I realized that he wasn't really going to do anything about my request, I decided to go to Marty myself.

I was only about fourteen years old at the time, but this didn't stop me from going for my goals. I went to Marty's shop on 161st and Jamaica Avenue and said to him, "Hey! Marlon is my friend, and he told me to ask you for a chair to work." Marty didn't turn me down. In fact, he told me to come around the shop for a little while to watch the other barbers cut, and when I felt I was ready, he'd give me a chair. So, after school every Tuesday for six months, I would go to the barbershop and watch the barbers do their thing. I would then take the things I had seen them do and go back home to practice it on my brother. I was literally pushing Todd's hairline back and making marks on his neck with the clipper. (He was like the guinea pig for my learning then.)

Over time, I was getting better and better at cutting and increasing my barbering skills. After six months of learning, I asked Marty if I could get a chair at the barbershop and he replied, "Yes."

Wisdom and Understanding Note

Never be afraid to step up and sell yourself. I'm still good friends with Marlon today. However, I wasn't going to let the fact that he didn't ask Marty to stop me from looking into the opportunity for myself. It's always good to do things the respectful way by first getting an introduction, but you may have to make contact and introduce yourself.

I was around fifteen when I started at Marty's shop, and every cut I did was a decent cut. I never had a client complain, nor did I ever mess anyone's hair up. At first, it was tough because people were skeptical about letting the new guy cut their hair, especially one so young, but by age sixteen, I was doing well enough to be making $500 to $600 a week cutting hair in that shop after school. I started spending some of this money on dumb stuff. I was buying gold chains and wearing some really nice clothes to the extent that some concerned folks started going to my mother to ask if I was selling drugs. To this day, I can honestly say that I never sold drugs to get money. Later, I did let my ambition influence me to try some other things, but never took the route of selling drugs.

CHAPTER 2

I THINK I AM AN ENTREPRENEUR

By age sixteen, I had started to grow as a barber and was making around $500 - $600 a week. For the next two years, I was cutting hair part-time, Monday through Friday after school. On Saturdays, I'd cut hair all day. As I continued to get better and better at my craft, my clientele grew bigger and bigger. I basically continued at that pace until I turned eighteen.

Right after my eighteenth birthday, an opportunity opened. A client at the barbershop named Opie had opened a new barbershop for a guy named Junior, who was a barber in the shop where I worked. Junior got himself into some trouble and was indicted and sent to jail shortly after their grand opening. The other barbers working at the new shop didn't last long either, leaving Opie with a barbershop and no barbers. Opie was in a bad position and needed to find new barbers immediately. The new barbershop was located on Hillside Ave and Parsons Boulevard in Queens, which was only about four blocks away from the shop where I worked. Opie came down to our shop to ask the manager if there were any barbers who would be interested in starting at the shop he had just opened. I was still a teenager, but there were a lot of bad things going on in Marty's shop I didn't particularly agree with. Yes, the money was good, but too much violence and other bad vices were beginning to become rampant in and around the shop.

> **Wisdom and Understanding Note**
>
> When you are looking to start a business that requires a specialty skill (Trade Skill), always have in mind the possibility of all your workers walking out. What will you do? It's not wise to open a small business in which you have to depend on other people's skills to make the business work. I share this advice with many people who ask me if they should open a barbershop. My answer is, "Only if you know how to cut hair." This way, if your entire staff decides to walk out, you will not have to suffer as much because you can pick up the slack. On the other hand, if you decide to open a business with a system that the average Joe could follow, then your workforce can be easily replaced. Make sure you know the difference and don't put yourself in a position like Opie.

There were about six barbers--including me, who worked at Marty's shop at the time, and because of the amount of money we were making, none of us really wanted to leave. When Opie came asking the second time, something in me clicked. At that moment, I realized that, although I could lose money, deep down I also wanted a change. I actually had no fear about the move. I knew I had some clients who would follow me, and it was an opportunity to see what could possibly happen. So, I decided to take the chance, not really knowing what the outcome would be. I sent a message to Opie and told him I would come around to the new shop the following week to cut hair.

Wisdom and Understanding Note

To this day, I often think about the decision I made when I was just eighteen to make this move. I remember how all the other barbers were saying, "Don't go." I remember saying to myself, If it fails or if it turns out bad, I can just come back. Never be afraid to see for yourself what the possibilities are for you.

At the end of the first week, I made just a little over $300. I wasn't discouraged with the drop because I knew many of my regular clients didn't know where I had relocated to on such short notice. My brother, Todd, who also was cutting hair at Marty's, started telling many of my clients where I was when they came for their haircuts. Some came to visit me, and others stayed at Marty's and used the other barbers. I knew that would probably be the case when I left but was still willing to take a chance at the new barbershop.

Wisdom and Understanding Note

Always have confidence in yourself. The more confidence you have in yourself, the more you will be rewarded for your actions.

JANUARY 2020

I TOOK A RIDE TO QUEENS NY TO LOCATE MARTY

THIS IS THE GUY THAT HIRED ME AT 15 YEARS OLD TO WORK IN HIS BARBERSHOP IN 1990 HE ALSO FIRED MY BROTHER...LOL

After the first month, I started averaging around $1000 and above every week. New clients were showing up, and some of my old ones were coming around, too, so business was booming. Opie started to get really excited; for the first time, he had a dedicated barber in the shop. He was making money and I didn't steal from him--unlike the other barbers prior to me. In fact, to build Opie's confidence in me running the barbershop, I gave him more than I actually owed him. On a few occasions, I would add a few extra hundreds to the commissions. I did this because I knew that, prior to me starting with him, he had been very discouraged about the success of that business. That effort on my part changed his entire outlook on the business.

Seed Note - I didn't know it at the time, but when I was giving Opie extra money above what I owed him, I was sowing the seed of overflow. It's one thing to pay what you owe, but another to give beyond. Even if you conduct a spiritual principle without knowing, it must work because it is a set law by God.

Opie grew fond of me and was taking more of a liking to me as he started to see the shop grow. My brother, Todd, joined me at the new shop about two months after I started there. Marty basically fired my brother because he found out he was telling my clients where my new location was.

Wisdom and Understanding Note

In the early 90's, cell phones were not yet that popular. Many of my clients only used the barbershop phone number to contact me. However, today, there are so many forms of technology to keep up with your client base. Keep client contacts so you can update them with all your business moves.

Six months into working at the new shop, I thought everything was going smoothly. So, imagine my surprise when the shop's landlord came around to tell me the shop owed almost four months' rent! I was shocked. I was paying Opie $600 - $800 weekly, which was more than enough money to cover the rent and have enough left over for profit. Finding out he was behind on the rent caught me completely off guard.

I told the landlord that I would try to get a hold of Opie, but he was nowhere to be found. For the next two weeks, I tried calling him five to six times a day. Still no Opie. This didn't stop the landlord from coming into the shop every other day looking for him. Here I was, making more than $1000 per week, and I was about to be evicted because someone didn't pay the rent. I could no longer make any excuses for Opie, and I tried to figure out what I could possibly do. I know my brother, Todd, must have asked me a dozen times, "Allen, what are we going to do?" After some thought, I said, "Next time the landlord comes into the shop, I'm going to plead my case to him." So, I did. I basically told him I have been here at the shop, building it up for the last six months and that I had been giving Opie $600 - $800 a week in commissions. Then he told me that the rent was only $1400 a month. I felt relief. I was convinced that I could manage and own the barbershop as my own. The next step would be getting the shop legally in my name.

I had to wait for the landlord to follow due process. He planned to serve Opie with eviction papers according to law, and afterward, I could rent the same shop at the same price. However, Opie was nowhere to be found. Through the court, the landlord was able to repossess his property, along with all the contents, in the barbershop.

Wisdom and Understanding Note

Some people would have walked away and not looked for an opportunity in this situation. Someone else's loss can possibly be

> your gain. Look at it this way: If you find yourself in a problem situation, look for the blessing and opportunity in it.

The deal the landlord gave me was to pay off the back rent, put down three months' security, and pay the first-month rent. After everything was said and done, I needed about $9800 to close the deal. I paid some from my personal savings upfront for the shop and borrowed $6500 more from my cousin, Michele's boyfriend (Will), to pay the rest.

I was eighteen around this time, and I had yet to develop disciplined saving habits, hence the reason I needed to take a loan to complete the payment for the shop. Finally, the shop was in my name. I had the papers, and everything seemed calm and settled again. Just two weeks later, Opie showed up to ask for his money for the last two months. Since I already paid up his debt, I told him point-blank that the shop was no longer in his name, and he didn't have any right to ask for anything.

Opie ran toward me and tried to put his hands around my neck. I ended up throwing him across the barbershop floor, and his head got stuck in the wall. His two brothers had to help him pull it out. I told Opie before he continued to talk to me, he'd better go on the roof and speak with the landlord, who was up there making repairs.

After his meeting with the landlord, Opie came back to me to ask how much I wanted to buy the barbershop for. I stood my ground and insisted that he had already lost everything since he had been evicted, and I wasn't paying him for anything. Opie left and that was the last day I ever saw him. That was how I got my first official barbershop business at age eighteen. I paid Will back $1000 a month and was extremely grateful for the loan.

When I think about it now, I realize none of it could have happened if I hadn't decided to go for the change. Now I realize this was kind of a pattern in my life. I really don't know what it is in me, but to this day, once I have my mind made up, I'm going to move forward regardless of what I have to go through. It's the reason why I get many of the results I get.

One day, a few months after I acquired the shop, a client came in who was a born-again Christian. He asked if I was saved, which only confused me because I didn't even know what he was talking about. When he found out I was eighteen and the owner of the shop, he said, "So, you are an entrepreneur." That was the first time I heard the term; so I questioned him about it. When he explained it, I realized I was exactly that--an entrepreneur.

Despite my success, I was confused about what career I wanted to pursue. Although I owned the shop, my father was on my back to get a "normal" nine to five job with benefits. He didn't really understand the entrepreneurial mindset and felt I wasn't taking my future seriously by depending solely on the barbershop. Ironically, I was already in love with the independence of being my own boss. No "regular" job could ever offer me that feeling.

Wisdom and Understanding Note

You will only live a fulfilling life doing the things that you love to do. For me, it's being my own boss and building things up. You may not care to be a boss, but make sure that whatever you

> do, you love doing it, or you will be doing a disservice to your life.

Through the process of evicting Opie and helping me get the shop in my name, my landlord and I got closer. He saw my perseverance and dedication and became my first millionaire mentor, sharing some important lessons with me. I will never forget those lessons as they helped propel the growth of the millionaire mindset that I was already building.

For example, I was always dressed nicely. I had a sneaker for every day of the week, and someone could have mistaken me for a rich person. My landlord, on the other hand, didn't dress as lavishly as I did but had millions. The building where my barber shop was located had thirteen occupied stores, which included a grocery store, my barbershop, a beauty salon, two restaurants, and a dentist office. My landlord was collecting around $40,000 in total rent from this building each month.

One time, he shared with me: "You come to your shop to make money. You are your own boss, and you show up at your business every day. But I show up to my building once a month, and my building is doing the work for me." I will never forget those words as they were my first lessons. This was the first time I had a millionaire share something with me personally, and it was the concept of leverage.

Leverage is basically using other people, things, or systems to make your money for you. I learned this valuable lesson in 1993 from my landlord. Here was a man who wore almost the same thing every day, but he was making money because people had to rent his stores. I, on the other hand, was spending a lot on jewelry and other fashion items that weren't making me anything in return. After this lesson, I didn't really care about having a luxury lifestyle as much. I'd rather have assets making me money than have five or ten pairs of sneakers making me nothing.

Wisdom and Understanding Note

If you don't have millionaire mentors, it would be a good idea to connect with as many as you could. It's one thing to read books; however, when you have someone you can call to get wise counsel, it's like having a cheat sheet for life's problems. The answers to where you are trying to go are the same ones they had to figure out to get to where they are. Just remember, never ask them for money. Just ask them for their WISDOM!

CHAPTER 3

HUSTLE TO HUSTLE

    After some time running the barbershop, I continued to try my hand at other new ways to make money. Sometimes I would sit for hours to think about how I could grow bigger in business. One day, while I was sitting in my barbershop, my friend, Greg, stopped by. Greg was a person who I could always talk to when it came to trying to make big moves. Greg had just come from the bookstore to give me a book that he purchased called "Think and Grow Rich" by Napoleon Hill. I have to be honest and say that I never was into reading books. Up until that point, I had never read a book from cover to cover, even with already having my high school diploma. Well, this was about to change in 1994.

    This book that Greg gave me was nothing that I would have purchased on my own. I put it in my clipper bag and that was where it remained for the next 3-4 weeks. I would simply leave it there while I would transport my clippers back and forth. One day, after about four weeks, I decided to clean out my clipper bag. I removed everything, including the book, which had found its way to the bottom of the bag. I'm not 100% sure what made me decide to open the book that night after ignoring it for so long, but I can say for sure that I'm glad I did. It was the first book in my life that I have read from cover to cover. Yes, I graduated high school and have completed many book reports; however, I had still never read a book in full. However, the content of this book opened my eyes to confirm some things about myself that I never saw in words before. It also introduced me to new ways of thinking. It was from that book that I started building a massive library of self-help, motivational, and business books that help to shape my way of thinking moving forward.

THE BEATS DROVE ME CRAZY

For as long as I can remember, I have always been into music. I would visit my uncle AD's home where he had a piano in his hallway. I remember plenty of times the other kids would invite me to play video games, or join them outside, but I would stay on that piano and continue to make melodies.

Then there was the time that my friend, Michael Simpson, had his older brother's keyboard. When I saw that keyboard, I asked him if I could borrow it for a couple of days. Those two days turned into a month of me just making music and beats.

The first keyboard I ever purchased came from my friend, Jonathan. Jonathan had a mini studio in his basement. It was the first time I saw someone with professional equipment making music & beats. I spent a couple of days at his home after work learning the equipment. Jonathan wanted to upgrade to some new equipment, so he asked me if I wanted to purchase one of his keyboards. We agreed on $700, and I became the owner of my first piece of music equipment.

It was at this time I envisioned myself making money in the music production business. I started to learn everything about my first piece of equipment and every month, I would buy a new piece. Before I knew it, I had a full studio that consisted of two mixing boards, drum machines, sound processors, and microphones. I started letting the kids in my neighborhood know that I was building a music studio.

The first person I worked with was my friend, Damion. I reached out to Damion because I knew he had been recording music with another friend of mine. I let him know I had a studio in my basement and we eventually created a group called Unforgiven. As I started to make demo tapes, I quickly noticed my sound quality needed improvement. I shared my feelings with one of the clients that used to come to my barbershop, who was also a music producer. He recommended that I enroll in an audio engineering school. I took his advice and enrolled myself in an audio engineering school in Smithtown, Long Island, New York. Immediately after being in school for a few months, my recording sound improved. Now, with that quality of music, I started to get more rappers wanting me to do music for them.

Eventually, my parents complained about the music being too loud in the basement. I had no choice but to look for a new place to build my studio. At the time, I had a little space in the back of my barbershop. With permission from the landlord, I moved the music studio into the back of the barbershop. It was not long after that I started charging hourly rates to help record local artists.

After some time, I started to realize that I was making a significant investment in my craft, equipment, and my time to help many of the artists I was working with. I was producing music for the artist that didn't have any money. Overall, I was providing a production studio for free. On a few occasions, I paid for marketing materials and created audio duplications for a few groups. I wanted to get more serious about it and felt the need to have contracts to protect myself.

I went to find a music business attorney and paid him $500.00 to develop music production contracts for my company. I also incorporated my company. This made me feel like a legitimate production company and helped me feel secure in putting all my time and money into those particular projects.

I went on to present these contracts to the artists I was working with. I found the artists who were not paying me did not want to commit to contracts. I had already spent about $3,000.00 of my own money to help promote the groups. I felt like I needed to have all the artists under contract in the event they were offered a record label deal. However, they did not see it like that. It was from that day I stopped working with any artist that didn't pay.

Wisdom and Understanding Note

Before you invest your time in others, make sure to have a proper commitment which, many times, is backed up by legal paperwork—Contracts!

From that time on, I changed my philosophy on how I was going to do music business. If you wanted my music production from that point on, you would need to make an advance payment.

A guy named Goongie was coming to my barbershop to get his haircut. Goongie's brother was a rapper and he was his manager.

He found out I was making beats and asked if I had any for sale. He let me hear some of his brother's music and he was actually good. After listening to a few of my beats, Goongie was impressed. There was one beat in particular that he loved and when his brother heard it, he wanted to rap on it!

Now, because of what I went through before, I made sure he knew he would have to pay for the beat upfront. We negotiated and he paid me $500.00 upfront for the production and we made a deal on back-end points if the song was to sell. Once I got the $500.00 for the beat, he made an appointment at D&D Studios in Manhattan where his brother recorded the song.

Somehow, the rapper, Fat Joe, heard the song. Goongie came back to me and told me that Fat Joe loved the song and wanted to meet the music producer who made the beat. We decided to meet in a music studio in Staten Island. Goongie told me to bring some beats to play for him.

Fat Joe was the first famous rapper to request to hear my beats. I felt like I had to put up my best when going for this meeting to present my beats. I wanted the beats that I was going to play for him to be extremely good. So, I locked myself in my studio just for a day to get some motivation. I listened to beats by DJ Premier, my favorite producer at the time, all day long. Once I was motivated and, in a mindset, to make music, I worked on a beat for the Fat Joe meeting.

The next day, I had three beats and was ready to head for the studio in Staten Island that evening. When I got to the studio, Goongie was there to meet me. We proceeded to enter the studio where Fat Joe was located.

I was introduced to Fat Joe and a new artist sitting next to him, an artist the hip hop world would soon know as Big Punisher (Big Pun). They complimented me on the beat I did for Goongie's brother and asked me if I was ready to play some more beats for them. It was at that time I handed over a tape to Fat Joe and he put it in the tape deck to play. Immediately, I knew they liked the music because they were bopping their heads really hard; but after listening to the second beat, Fat Joe stopped the tape. He said, "The music was very good, but they sound like DJ Premier made them." He told me if he wanted music production from DJ Premier, he would have just called DJ Premier to the studio. I felt like I blew the opportunity. The music I was listening to for motivation was good, but I let it influence me instead of believing I could be my own inspiration. On my way home, I was totally disappointed that I did not believe enough in myself.

Wisdom and Understanding Note

It's great to have things in our lives to inspire us. However, you can't allow it to cover your own creativity. Whenever I'm looking to be creative or have a new project that requires me to do something new, I look into myself to be unique and to produce what makes me feel good. I also try to make sure that whatever I do has not been done before. I use this moment in the studio with Fat Joe and Big Pun as a life lesson to live by.

Nothing in the music business took off for me at that time. After about a year, I decided to fall back from it and focus on a few other things. I was meeting a lot of other rappers, independent and famous. During this time, I learned a lot; from audio engineering to contracts, to dealing with people in the business. However, the time spent on it was not paying off as I needed it to.

JUST A LITTLE STRIPPING AND WAXING

It was a short time after owning my first barbershop that I needed my floors done. So, I found a guy to do my floors. I was always one to be very observant, so I watched each step of the process. At that time, I was always looking for ways to make more money, so I asked him how much the buffing machine cost. He said about $1,200 for a brand new one. I thought I could get my own buffing machine and do my own floors instead of paying $200.00 each time he did it.

I started to look around to see if I could find a used buffing machine. Not too far from me, on Queens Blvd, I located a hardware store that sold used buffing machines. So, I went and discovered they had used buffing machines for $200.00, and I purchased one.

The next time I needed my floors done, I did them myself. My brother and I started a floor stripping & waxing business. It was called Brown Brothers Cleaning Company. What we did to start growing the business was to ask local business owners if they needed their floors done. The first account we received was a check-cashing place down the street from the barbershop. After getting that first contract, the owner told us he had two other check-cashing stores. We ended up getting another account in Harlem. The money was good, but it would be very time consuming to grow the cleaning business ourselves while at the same time, running the barbershop. My brother no longer wanted to do the cleaning business, so he decided to pull out, and I started to see it was becoming a bit time-consuming. I decided to throw in the towel.

> **Wisdom and Understanding Note**
>
> Just because some businesses may be easy to get started, it doesn't mean it is the right business for you to take on. As I grew in business over the years, I started to discover that there are different levels of entrepreneurship. Keep reading and you will start to understand what I mean.

ILLEGALLY PARKED CARS

Next to my barbershop, there was a parking lot that belonged to the owner of the building I was renting from. The landlord hired a company to boot cars that illegally parked on his property. The problem was the company was not there many of the times when cars were parked illegally. The landlord expressed his frustration to me and that's when I decided to start my own booting company.

I had developed a relationship with the previous guys who were hired by the landlord. One of my friends named Henry came home from prison needing a job. So, I spoke to Ralph, the owner of the booting company, to see if he would give Henry a job. Ralph hired Henry about a week later. As a result, I got to learn more about how to boot cars and the booting business.

Ralph's business started to grow elsewhere, so he could no longer pay attention to the parking lot next to the barbershop. When the landlord expressed his need to me, I told him to give me a couple of weeks and I could take over the lot for him. He said yes and gave me the contract for that lot.

> ### Wisdom and Understanding Note
>
> Many entrepreneurs spend lots of money upfront before they are even sure they can get any clients. I'm not saying it's wrong to do so. However, if you can secure your clients before you even make the first investment, it's way more possible you will succeed. In this particular deal, I secured the contract first and then, made the investment. This method may not apply for every business or service, but whenever you can test the waters first or secure a deal before you spend money, *Do It!*

The next day, I went to Coney Island to talk to Ralph at one of his lots and asked him what I needed to start my own booting company. At first, he was kind of hesitant as if not to give me any information. But I kept pressing him until he told me where he purchased the car boots from and where to receive the booting license from. After a while, he told me that I needed my own corporation and that the Department of Consumer Affairs would give me a license. Since I already had my music production corporation, I did not need to start a new company. I simply did a DBA (Doing Business As) and named it Good Guy Parking Enforcement. Within two weeks' time, I had my booting company license from the Department of Consumer Affairs. My brother and I ordered two boots from Canada that cost $450.00 each to start. The first day the boots were delivered, we booted six cars. The boot release fee was $100.00 plus tax, so you can see how this business had great potential. The great thing about this business was that I was able to hire many of my friends. We paid each person $25.00 for each car they placed a boot on. The remaining $75.00 went to the company.

On average, we would do about fifteen to twenty cars weekly at that location. I started to see the potential and wanted it to grow bigger by getting other lots. I had a friend of mine who worked beside a McDonalds. He saw the money we were making and suggested maybe we could be partners because he knew the owner of McDonald's. The owner had the same problem as my landlord. Cars would park illegally on a daily basis. So, after a few talks and adding one more of my friends to the business, we had a new deal. This turned out to be a good deal because the McDonald's parking lot, on average, did six to eight cars per day during the week. From there, we were able to secure a few more lots and the business was growing to the point we were all able to make good money. Things were going pretty well in this business but that was all about to change.

SUMMER 1997

BROWN BROTHERS BARBER SHOP
TOP RIGHT

MY FIRST PARKING LOT TO THE LEFT OF THE SHOP
GOOD GUY PARKING ENFORCEMENT STARTED THERE

THE WHITE VAN IN FRONT WAS USED FOR MY
FLOOR CLEANING BUSINESS

CHAPTER 4

I AM NEVER GETTING MARRIED

I was doing well for myself at a young age. I had a few businesses and since I was making more money than most of my friends, I'd often take them out to clubs and settle the bills. I don't regret any of those moments—in fact, I am glad I indulged in those activities at an early age. I believe it helped me get it out of my system rather than continuing to do childish things as I grew older. **"When I was a child, I spoke as a child, I understood as a child, I thought as a child: but when I became a man, I put away childish things." 1 Corinthians 13:11**

One day while I was conducting business as usual, a fine young lady parked her Mercedes Benz—illegally of course—at one of the parking lots my company managed. As was the normal practice, her car was booted. When she discovered this, she came to the office and requested to see the person in charge. During our conversation, I vividly remember her asking, "Sir, if I was your wife, would you keep my car locked up like this?" I replied, "One, you are not my wife, and two, I am not looking to get married anytime soon. I am only twenty-two years old and not looking to get married until

I'm in my thirties." My reply must have been a surprise to her because her eyes widened in shock. When she recovered, she asked if I meant what I said, and I replied, "Yeah, so you have to pay up the $100 plus tax to get your car released." She got the message because she stopped trying to get over on me and left to get the money. A pretty face and a Mercedes Benz didn't mean free to me. I had meant what I said. I wasn't getting married any time soon. It was my current state of mind, but someone was about to change it.

    The following week, I was driving my van, loaded up with DJ equipment—speakers, mixers, records, etc.—headed to my mother's job. My mother had asked if I could come and DJ at a party for unfortunate kids at her job. I arrived early to set up my equipment and did a little bit of soundcheck. I told my mother that I needed to go somewhere and that I would be back before the party started. My mother asked if I could drop-off two young ladies who were co-workers, and I obliged immediately. At first, I was thinking I would probably talk to whichever of the ladies that caught my eye, but as we left, I changed my mind. I already had a few women I was dealing with at that time. Even though I was only twenty-two, I was tired of just going after women that I really didn't have much interest in, just to be doing it. I remember while I was driving them, I said a prayer: "God, I just really need to find one woman, a woman I can build with."

    After I dropped the girls off, I started to make a U-turn and then changed my mind. It felt like something wanted me to go up two blocks to the Long Island Expressway. I obeyed the voice in my head, drove up the Long Island Expressway, and then made a left on Main Street.

As I drove, I came through the intersection at 73rd Avenue. I saw a pretty young lady walking down the street, and somehow, we made eye contact. I smiled at her and she smiled back, so I looked at her and said while gesticulating, "Can I make a U-turn and talk to you?" Since she was still smiling, I decided to make that turn and talk to her. I made the turn so fast that she didn't even notice me come up behind her. When I rolled my window down and said, "Hey! How are you doing?" she looked quickly back to reply. I realized at that moment, that she was only being receptive because she initially thought I was someone she knew, but now seeing me up close and personal, she realized she was mistaken. I discovered later that the person she thought I was had gone to high school with me, and we were often thought to be brothers. She had grown up in the same neighborhood as him some years ago.

We started talking, and I asked her where she was headed. After she told me she was going to the train station to catch the train to her sister's place in Brooklyn, I told her I was headed that way, too, and asked if I could drop her off. I honestly was going that route. I didn't want her to panic at the offer since I was, technically, a stranger. I explained to her that my shop was that way, and I was only offering my help because she seemed like a nice, young lady. She agreed and got in the car. I could tell that she wasn't totally comfortable, though, because she was leaning so close to the door. The tension in the car eased up five minutes later, and she began to chat more freely with me. We were getting to know each other by making normal small talk. We came up to my shop, and I quickly ran inside to tell my brother that I would be back a little later.

Prior to this time, I had been meeting other females, but there was nothing special or extraordinary. Things felt different with her almost immediately. Here I was, engaged in a conversation with this girl I just met, and we were driving to the train station. I was thinking she was just another girl—I had forgotten about my earlier prayer—but as we went on, I realized that I really liked her. We were coming up to the train station, but I wanted to continue the conversation and offered to drive her to her sister's house. She initially objected, but due to my persistence and the good conversation, we went on driving.

When we got to her sister's house, we talked for a little while. I told her that I needed to get back to work, and she said, "Okay." She glanced at my hands and noticed that they were a little dry and ashy. With a smile, she told me that she had some lotion. I really didn't know what to think of that, and laughed nervously. I thought she was going to hand me some lotion from her bag, but I was wrong. She took some Victoria Secret lotion out of her bag, squeezed it onto her hands, and proceeded to rub the lotion all over my hands. I remember feeling good inside as I watched her. When she finished, I thanked her, and I knew at that moment that she had just completely taken my heart.

As I was about to leave, I intentionally did not ask for her phone number. I wanted to see if she would ask me for mine. I had to know if she was really interested in me. I said, "I guess I will see you later." She looked kind of puzzled and said, "How will you contact me when you don't have my number?" At that point, I was definitely digging her. I played it off and said, "Oh yeah, I forgot about that." Then, I asked her for her number.

Now I had her number, and we parted ways. On my drive back to the barbershop, I couldn't stop smelling my hands and saying to myself, *This Victoria Secret smells so good.* By the time I got to the shop, I was on cloud nine. I looked at my brother and I said, "Yo bro, I think I just found my wife!" He noticed the excitement in my voice and the radiance in my face, and he asked me what was up. I didn't even think twice before I replied. I said, "Todd, I think I just met my wife." He must have thought I was joking because he chuckled and asked if I was serious. I sat on the speaker underneath the payphone that we had in the shop and kept sniffing the Victoria Secret on my hand.

I didn't call her the next day because I didn't want to seem desperate. I waited one more day. I found out, years later, that she was a bit upset about that because she had anticipated I would call the following day. She had her hair done nicely but decided to undo it because I didn't call her. I set up a date for us to go out and have dinner. We went to eat, then to play pool and for the next nine days, we went out every night. There was barely any physical contact all through this period, let alone any form of intimacy. The only thing that happened was on day six. At the entrance of her home was a long path. Since I didn't feel like walking the long way, I decided to take the short cut across the grass. She had told me she didn't like to walk in the grass, so I picked her up across my chest, holding her with both my arms out as I proceeded to carry her across. About halfway across, she looked at me and we made eye contact. I went in for our first kiss. She turned towards me and put her arms around my neck, and we kissed as I carried her the rest of the way to her door. It was kind of magical. By day seven, I was already head over heels in love with Melissa. She had begun to share some of her personal stories, and I did likewise, and this was what we did every single day.

I was in love no doubt, and this feeling was becoming so overwhelming that I concluded that I was going to marry her. It got to the point where I couldn't eat because I would lose my appetite just thinking about her. I shared my plans with my brother Todd. After we talked, he said, "If you're sure about marriage, then it's up to you to do it." I began ring shopping almost immediately after this discussion. During one of my shopping trips, it crossed my mind that I had told another woman a few weeks back that I wasn't planning to get married anytime soon.

Wisdom and Understanding Note

Life has its way of putting you at a crossroads. The way you think one day could be challenged by the opportunities that present themselves to you the next day. You must know that you are not promised to have everything you want in your own timing. I have seen people who put off having kids only to pass the time and then can't have them when they thought it would be convenient for them for several reasons. I have seen the same for marriage. There is no guarantee that the right person will be there when you reach your thirties. One thing I have learned in this life is that it's okay to have plans, but when something or someone comes in your life, be willing to change your mind to take full advantage of opportunities. Don't take it for granted that you will have a chance later in life.

As the jeweler showed me different types of rings, he would say something like, "This ring is the type you buy for a girl you want to be with for only about a year." Then he showed me a bigger ring and said, "This ring is for a girl you'll want to stay with for fifteen to twenty years." Finally, he showed me a $5000 ring and said, "This is the type of ring you get for a girl that you want to be married to forever." I told him the forever ring was the ring I wanted. I immediately put down the $1,000 deposit and paid the remainder later. Now that I had the ring, I was nervous about what I was going to do next. The ring was just over a one-carat diamond and was packaged in a synthetic rose stem box. It was beautiful.

I called her up later that day to see what she was doing after work. She said that she was free, and I asked her if she wanted to go to Coney Island. She would be getting off work at 11 pm and that was the best place to pop the question--if it came down to it. The ring was tucked in my sock, and I was prepared to propose when we got to the park. We went to the arcade and had been playing games for a while when she suddenly turned to me and asked a strange question. "Would you ever get a tattoo?" she asked. I continued playing the game, but I wondered what had inspired her to ask about a tattoo. I told her that I hadn't planned on ever getting a tattoo, but if I were going to get a tattoo on my body, it would be my wife's name only. Her next statement was more surprising than the first. She said, "So you are going to get a tattoo that says, Melissa?" This was a confirmation to me because she had no way of knowing that I had the ring or that I was planning to propose that night.

I asked her to walk with me down to the boardwalk. That's where I popped the question. It was the classic old school style: I turned her around, got on one knee, and said something like, "These past eleven days have been amazing; I have never met anyone like you, and I want to be with you for the rest of my life. I know it's early, but I also know that I am meant to be with you forever. I love you."

It is important to note that we had only known each other for eleven days when I proposed. We met on June 5th, 1997 and I popped the question on June 16th, 1997. So, there we were, together on the boardwalk bench. I had just proposed after having gotten confirmation from the tattoo question she asked earlier that night…but she was looking at me in shock. I guess the event overwhelmed her a bit. Thankfully, after her long pause, she said, "Yes!" We were both nervous as we sat there, recovering from all that had just happened while we talked. We agreed that we were going to take things slowly and would stay engaged for two years to see how things went. It was now a reality. I was engaged, and I was on cloud nine.

The following morning, around 6:00, we got to my parent's house as my father was preparing to leave for work. My mother had only seen Melissa one time before then, and my dad had yet to meet her. When my father came down to see us, I remember saying, "Dad, this is my fiancé." He thought I was joking, so he just greeted her like he would greet any of my other friends, and then he left for work. When my mother came down later, I introduced Melissa to her as my fiancé. It threw my mother totally off guard. We stood there laughing with my mom and showed her the ring to let her know we weren't joking.

I later learned that my mom had called my dad to discuss the engagement. She later told me how the conversation went:

"Elijah, did Allen tell you he was engaged?"

"Yeah, he told me, but I just thought he was joking."

"Did you see the rock he put on that girl's finger...I mean, did you see the ring?"

"Wait...what!"

Funny right? Anyway, Dad called me up that afternoon just to confirm that I was serious about the whole engagement thing. I told him I was. Then Dad said, "What are you doing this afternoon? I need you to come over and have lunch with me." My father had never asked me to come over for lunch at his work before, so imagine my nervousness. I went over later that afternoon. As we sat at the table, he began to ask some questions concerning my fiancé. He wanted to know how long I had known her, and if I was certain that this was what I wanted to do. My mind was already made up at this time. I doubt that there was anything he could have said that would have changed it. I told him this was who I wanted, and that I wanted to be with her forever.

He tried to warn me. Actually, he advised me—and rightfully so—to take precautions because he felt I was rushing into something. I respect that he did this. Any reasonable father would have done the same in his shoes.

Wisdom and Understanding Note

Even though I decided not to listen to the wisdom that my dad was trying to share, it didn't mean he was wrong. I jumped in fast based on the strong emotions I was feeling. He was trying to tell me to get to know her a little more before I went all the way in. This works both ways. You can be with someone, discover that they are not perfect, and then decide to not move

> forward with them because of their flaws. But you may end up going from person to person looking for the perfect one that doesn't exist. When mature individuals enter a commitment, they have an incentive to work it out. The keyword is mature!

Aside from my parents, I remember telling my friends that I was engaged, and they all made jokes about it. I don't blame them, though. I was the type of guy who always expressed my love for the bachelor life. So, when I suddenly switched tunes and started talking about getting married, a lot of them thought it was probably because the sex was good, but that wasn't the truth at all. I put a ring on her finger before anything like that ever happened. In fact, it was a long time after engagement before any intimacy on that level happened between us.

Melissa has been so much of a blessing to me because a lot of the problems we went through were growing pains that helped develop me more. Her background was different from mine, and though we have had some falling outs through the course of the relationship, we stayed consistent. This consistency helped us come back better and stronger each time. There were times that it felt as if we were heading for the rocks and were almost calling for a divorce, but, as they say, love conquers all. One thing I always kept in mind was the fact that I had prayed before I got her, and I believed that God was the one who gave her to me. This thought helped me forge ahead. That thought continues to be part of the bond that keeps me going daily. I am blessed because she is basically a character builder for me. As I lived with her over time, the day to day events shaped my character. I am a better man because of her.

Wisdom and Understanding Note

Being in a barbershop affords you the opportunity to listen to all sorts of conversations covering many ranges of topics. One such conversation that sticks with me even now came from an older gentleman. He said something about how it was good for a young man to get married early. What he said was reasonable. Getting married early in life would help the young man get serious about life, be able to save money, allow the two of them to grow gradually together and plan things more efficiently, giving them plenty of time to accomplish goals. This conversation always stuck with me, and I had to add it as a wisdom note. I know there may be differences of opinion on this one, but getting married young can have many benefits. I will have to say that maturity in both individuals plays a crucial part as to whether it will work or not.

SHORT CUTS BARBER SHOP JULY 1997

SUMMER OF 1997
1 MONTH AFTER MEETING

CHAPTER 5

I ONCE WAS BLIND NOW I CAN SEE

Exactly a month after my engagement on June 16th, 1997, I opened a new barbershop with my fiancé, Melissa. This was my second barbershop and my friends were surprised that I put it in my fiancé's name. Some of them were worried if I could trust her and expressed their feelings to me, but because I was confident in our relationship, I had no worries about it. Besides, the shop cost around $9,000 to get started and $3,200 of it was money that she put in. Melissa quit her job and started managing the new shop while I managed the other one. We kept growing and learning more about each other as time went on.

MY FRIENDS WOULDN'T DO THAT TO ME

Shortly after I started this new business with my fiancé, things started to get a little sketchy with my partners in the booting business. Out of nowhere, Melissa came to me and told me she thought that my business partners were stealing money from me. I asked her where she had gotten that idea, but what she said next didn't make any sense to me. "I just feel it," she said. I was a little confused about the whole thing. I told her that I had known my partners for years. They wouldn't do that to me. I was also thinking that I had known her for less than four months. How could she say such a thing? She left it alone for a few weeks. Then she repeated her concerns. She said, "Something is not right with your business partners." The more I thought about it, the more I knew that I needed to do some checking on my partners. Melissa might just be right.

    A few months prior to this, my friend, Danny, was getting a divorce. His wife caught him cheating and wanted out of the relationship. She connected a recording device to their home phone, and that's how she found out that he was cheating on her. It was a little device you would get from Radio Shack that cost about $15. She would come home from work and listen to all the conversations her husband was having with other women while she was at work. Danny told the story in the barbershop one day. It gave me an idea. Because of what my fiancé was feeling, I decided to go to Radio Shack and grab one of those devices to hook up to the business line we had for the booting company. To my surprise, Melissa was right.

    I logged about two months' worth of calls. Many of them didn't reveal much, but there were seven or eight calls that told it all. The calls revealed the plot that my partners had come up with to take the business from me and to steal important documents out of my name. They had also plotted other movements to hide money from cash receivables so that I wouldn't know it was missing. As we went over the material, I remember my fiancé looking at me with the "I told you so" face. This was all a shock to me. How could I have been so blind to this? After all, I had known these two guys as friends first—at least I thought I did. After the shock of it all wore off a bit, I had to put a plan together to get them out or dissolve the business.

Now knowing that I was really dealing with shady individuals, I concluded that I would slowly try to pull my money out of the business. I decided to go this route because of the new information I had received. Days after I discovered their plot, the Department of Consumer Affairs sent out a letter to all booting companies in New York changing the rules and regulations governing the booting industry. The main change they were regulating was the price you could charge once someone was booted on private property. The boot release fee was $100 plus tax. With the new regulation change, it was going to be only $25, which would completely kill the business I had set up. Now, if I hadn't discovered the plot my partners had against me, I would have shared that news with them. However, because everything was in my name, I'm the only one that received the letter. I decided not to tell them anything.

PROCEED WITH CAUTION

It was going to be about four months until January 1, which was when the new rules and regulations were going to take effect. Time was limited, so I had to get out of the partnership before then. My partners had a history in Queens, and I was very aware of previous things they had done on the streets. In reality, I had never been bothered by it because I wasn't scared of them, but I know I wanted things to play out smoothly so as not to start a war with them.

While we were running the booting company, we would have a meeting every Tuesday night at one of the partners' houses. He was the only one who had a floor safe, so we kept company cash there. This was a mistake on my part, but remember, I trusted those guys. I continued moving forward with them as if I didn't know their secret plans. My plan was to get all I could out of the business and then dump it on them. It would soon have no value because of the new regulations. I also wanted to get my brother back the money he had invested into the business.

My brother had been pretty much a silent partner from the start, so my priority was to get him some of his money back. I called a meeting and made up a story that my brother wanted out, and we needed to buy out his percent of the business. This made sense to all of them and they agreed because it would give them more ownership. After that meeting, we handed Todd the cash and he was out. The next move was to have them buy my percent of the business. At the time, we had equipment assets and a large five-figure cash stash in the safe. My objective was to get as much of the safe cash as I could by selling them my ownership. This was the plan, but it didn't quite make it that far.

THE STRAW THAT BROKE THE CAMEL'S BACK

Around that time, I reviewed some of the recordings and heard something that was not going to allow me to just sit back and be cool anymore. Before then, I had heard them talk about my fiancée, about the money they were taking, their secret plans, and even things about me which were complete lies. None of it bothered me at all. They even expressed that they were mad that I had opened a new barbershop business with my fiancée and not them. That was funny to me. However, what did make me flip out was when I heard one of them say to the other that he was trying to locate my Social Security number so he could forge a document to get the booting company license out of my name. It was at that point that I went into full war mode.

That same day, I went to the hardware store and changed the locks on my store. The next day, my partner, who was the field manager, came and saw the locks to the office were changed. I'm sure he knew that I was on to them because no one tried to call me for a couple of days. Then a close friend of mine, who knows one of them, asked me about it. He said, "Hey Al, did you change the locks?" I responded, "Hell yes, and they better not come around here anymore." At that point, I didn't care about the plan nor getting into beef with any of them. As far as the money in the safe, I'm not sure what they did with it, but I didn't care. I'm almost sure they figured that if they talked with me, we would need to settle it or fight.

They had the money and my percentage, so they didn't want to see me. I learned, long ago, that people that owe you money and have no intention of paying it will avoid you. It cost me $30,000 plus whatever future earnings I could have negotiated, but I got rid of a major headache. What bothered me more than anything was knowing that I had put these guys into my business thinking they were my friends, only to discover they were more like wolves.

GOD GAVE ME THE RIGHT WOMAN

Melissa had been right about those guys the whole time. This had opened my eyes to her value in my life even more. I had only known her for a few months, but she was able to see something I couldn't see. This became an ongoing theme in our relationship. She seemed to be able to see things that I couldn't and would warn me of danger. Our love continued to grow stronger and stronger.

A song was released about this time that became one of my mother's favorites. The song was called "For You" by Kenny Lattimore. I had heard this song a few dozen times before I met

Melissa. After I met Melissa, my mother would say, "This song is made for you guys." She even suggested it be our wedding song. One day, as I was driving home by myself, the song came on the radio. It was the first time I had really listened to the words. By the time I reached home and pulled into my driveway, tears were falling down my face. I was just overwhelmed with joy that I could feel the way I did about her. The song was a perfect expression of how I felt about my future wife.

PHASE TWO

Life Knowing Jesus Christ

CHAPTER 6

HEARING GOD'S VOICE FOR THE FIRST TIME

The falling out with my booting partners happened at the end of November 1997. For a few months afterward, I would think about how the whole thing had gone down. I wondered how close friends, or just people in general, could disguise their motives. A few months after that incident, I had more falling outs with other individuals that forced me to change more of the dynamics of all my businesses. I really didn't know what was going on, but one thing was for sure; Melissa was right there with me the entire time supporting me.

It was April of 1998, and Easter had come around. Up until this point in our relationship, we hadn't attended church. I'm not exactly sure how it came up, but we both decided to go to Easter service. I decided that we would visit my parent's church, and Melissa was fine with that. As we were about to make a left turn from the intersection into the parking lot, Melissa changed her mind. She had decided we should go to another church instead. She had visited that church a year before she met me and suggested we attend there. I was all for it and proceeded to the Community Church of

Christ in Jamaica Queens, New York, pastored by Bishop Lester Williams.

As we arrived, we noticed the church was extremely crowded. This was Easter Sunday when people who normally wouldn't attend flooded the church. That day, we were also part of the once-a-year crowd. As the service went on, it appeared to be a normal worship service. There was singing, praising God, church announcements, offering, and then more singing and praising God. Then it was time for the preacher to preach the Word of God.

The pastor started preaching, and for the first time ever, I was following what a preacher was saying. I can't remember all the details because it happened over twenty years ago, but I remember that he kept repeating, "Jesus is the real deal." He started preaching about everything that had happened in my life in the previous months. Not that he was speaking directly to me or about me, but the points he was raising were in line with what I had been going through. I couldn't believe what I was hearing! I remember thinking *OMG! Is this preacher speaking to me or what?* At the end of the sermon, he invited anyone who was hearing God speaking to them to come forward and give their lives to Christ. At that moment, I heard the voice of God saying, "Come forward. I want to get to know you." I turned to Melissa and told her that I had to go up there. She asked if I was sure, reminding me this was something that required commitment. I was already convinced in my heart about this decision, so I told her I had to go. I walked to the front of the altar, and the pastor's wife, co-pastor Shirley G. Williams, she is a Bishop now-- signaled to me. When I went to meet her, she started praying over me. During the prayer, I could hear God speaking to me, and I was seeing beautiful colors and crying tears of joy. This was the most miraculous event that has happened to me thus far, and I cherished every single moment of it.

I got signed up to the ministry almost immediately, and I was enrolled in what was called the New Beginner's class. In this class, they taught about the Gospel and Jesus Christ, and they explained the principles of being a believer. Melissa and I started attending church every week, and I was learning new things daily. The church provided baptism services four times a year, and in June 1998, my future wife and I were baptized by our pastor.

PREACHING IN MY DREAM

The day after I was baptized, I woke up from a dream where I was preaching to a large crowd of about four hundred people. I remember waking up, wondering why in the world would I have that kind of dream. At this time, my fiancé's parents had moved to Georgia, so she was staying with my parents. As Christian parents, they insisted I stay in the basement while she stayed upstairs since we were not yet married. I ran upstairs and told Melissa about the dream. Neither of us thought too much of the dream, and at that point, didn't have a revelation as to the dreams' meaning. We had planned that day to go to a Christian bookstore to get some books and Christian audiotapes.

THE HOLY SPIRIT TOLD ME TO TELL YOU!

We decided to first go to the bike store to get new bikes, and we rode these bikes to the Christian bookstore. We were locking our bikes outside the Christian bookstore when this guy named Rev. Johnson walked out of the same store. I didn't know Rev. Johnson, but Melissa did because he was getting his hair cut at the shop she was managing. As he came out, they both exchanged greetings, and

Melissa introduced me to him as her fiancé. I stood with Rev. Johnson, and we had a little small talk before he announced that he had to leave. I was just about to walk into the bookstore with Melissa when he suddenly stopped walking and asked me to come back towards him. I walked up to him, and he said, "The Holy Spirit told me you are a preacher, and you don't even know it yet." This came as a surprise to me because I didn't really know much about the Holy Spirit yet, and I was wondering at the same time why the Holy Spirit would decide to tell Rev. Johnson something like that concerning me. The fact that I had a dream about preaching that morning, combined with Rev. Johnson saying the same thing, blew my mind. I wasn't one hundred percent sure yet, but it was just too real to be coincidental.

ARE YOU A PREACHER OR A MINISTER?

The following week, I went with Melissa to a restaurant in Long Island called Old Country Buffet. As we sat down, a young guy who appeared to be the coach of a baseball team came over to me and he said, "Let me ask you something. Are you a preacher or a minister?" I told him, "No." As he left, I thought about his question because of what had happened with Rev. Johnson and the dream the previous week. I finally concluded that it was a mere coincidence. Some days later, I was sitting in my barbershop when another guy walked in and he said, "Hey Preacher, come cut my hair?" Wow! This couldn't be just a coincidence anymore. I asked him why he called me "Preacher." He told me that there wasn't any specific reason other than he thought I looked like a preacher based on the way I was sitting when he walked in.

Barely a week after this, I went with Melissa to the old country buffet restaurant again. It just so happened the host sat us at the same booth where we had sat two weeks earlier. A black guy, accompanied by a lady, came to sit at the booth next to us. Trying to make small talk, he asked if I was a preacher or a minister. Things were beginning to get spooky. The following week, I was heading to the barbershop, and as I crossed the street, one guy waved and greeted me with the words "What's up, preacher?" I had to admit that there was something about all this, but in the back of my mind, I was still trying to convince myself that it was all just a coincidence.

The following week, I wanted to go to Green Acres Mall in Queens to get shoes for church, so Melissa and I decided to take the city bus from Jamaica Avenue and Parsons Boulevard instead of driving. As we got on the bus, I told Melissa that I wanted to sit in the front, but she said she'll prefer the back seats. I was able to persuade her, and we finally moved to sit up front in the granny seats. (We called the front seats granny seats because that was where the old folks loved to sit.) Halfway through the trip, when we were almost at the Green Acres Mall, the bus driver suddenly turned and looked at me. He asked the same question that people had been asking me for the last six weeks. When I heard the "Are you a preacher or something?", I thought, *here we go again.* Melissa sat there smiling at me because I had told her about all the other incidents, and she had experienced it herself three other times with me at the restaurant, and the one time at the Christian bookstore. The bus driver continued talking and said that he had a brother in North Carolina who was a preacher and that I reminded him of that person. As we drove on, I looked over to the left, almost at the same time as the driver, and he pointed to a big building on the side of the road and said, "You see that building over there? You are going to have a church that big someday." I was perplexed. Here was another person who didn't know me at all, yet he was speaking into my life as if he knew something I didn't.

GOD IS TRYING TO TELL YOU SOMETHING

Things like this kept happening, so I went to my pastor to seek his advice. I told him about how I always seemed to be running into someone who thought I was a minister or a preacher. I wanted to know what he thought about it all. He said that God was trying to tell me something and that was why He kept sending people to me. I called my mother afterward to see if she was home and went to visit her. I shared everything that had been happening to me and asked her opinion. My mom replied by telling me a story about something that had happened when I was younger. She was taking my siblings and me to church one Sunday. Our neighbor, who lived a few houses down, came up to her and complimented everyone on how nice they looked. When she went on to compliment me, she said, "Allen looks nice, but when he grows up, he is going to be a minister." I sat there with my mouth wide open in surprise. I asked my mother why this was the first time I had heard this story. Her only reply was that she had forgotten the story until now and had only remembered it because of what I had told her. After speaking with my mother that day, I was convinced this was no longer a coincidence.

YES LORD - I WILL PREACH YOUR WORD

The following week, I attended a tent service where Prophet Andre Cook was preaching. This was the first time I had ever seen this preacher. He was preaching from the book of Luke about Jesus' first encounter with Peter at the river. Jesus told Peter that He would make him a fisher of men. I remember that sermon like it was yesterday because it still carries so much significance to me. At the end of the service, Prophet Cook began to prophesy over people. At some point, he called me from the back and asked me to come to the front of the church. He also signaled for Melissa to come up front and stand beside me. He said that random people had been coming up to ask me if I was a preacher or minister and that it wouldn't stop until I accepted the call on my life to be a minister and preach God's Word. As he was saying this, I turned to my fiancé, and she was crying. She was so touched because, in the thirteen weeks of random people coming to me confirming what God was saying to me, she had been right there beside me five or six times. When the minister was finished prophesying to us, he laid his hands on us and prayed for both of us. We both fell under that anointing, and I remember that I was down on the floor, asking myself what had happened. This happened on the thirteenth week after people had been coming up to me asking if I was a minister or a preacher. I remember as I lay on the ground, I kept saying, "Yes Lord, I'll preach your word." It is interesting to note, from that day when I accepted God's call on my life until today, no one has randomly come up to me and asked that question again.

After this service, I immediately accepted the call to be a preacher and enrolled in the ministry program at Church. I began to make gradual progress in the ministry. This was where I discovered that the Holy Spirit had different ways of speaking to me and confirming His word through random people. He has done this on several occasions, but I'll talk more about this later.

SHORT CUTS BARBER SHOP JUNE 1998
I CHANGED THE WINDOW SIGN ONCE I ACCEPTED JESUS CHRIST
"JESUS LOVE YOU ~ CHRISTIAN BARBER SHOP"

CHAPTER 7

LEARNING TO TRUST GOD'S TIMING

When God called me into the ministry to preach, the first revelation He gave me was through a dream. As you may recall from the previous chapter after the dream came a series of confirmations. Random people, my mother, Bishop Williams, and Prophet Andre Cook all offered me confirmation of what God wanted me to do. So I was pretty much clear on the direction I should take. I was pretty excited to know that God works in such away. Through the dream I had, God showed me how he wanted me to preach and teach His word.

ENROLLING IN NEW MINISTER'S CLASS

My pastor told me that I should enroll in the next minister's training class. The class was basically a two-year training program where new ministers were educated about the ministry, and then issued a minister's license as a lay minister after completion. After the initial training, the new lay minister must work for another two years in the church before being able to qualify to be ordained as an elder. It's at this point that one becomes an ordained minister in this particular church organization. I figured in 4 to 5 years, I would be an ordained minister and doing what God called me to do. I was 100 percent cool with this and ready to go through the learning process.

The following January, I enrolled in the ministry class, alongside some other folks, and I was so excited to begin. I was elated to be moving forward as a Christian and honored that God would want me to be a minister of His Gospel. I began to move up the ladder in church leadership quickly. While I was waiting for the minister classes to begin, my pastor had taken note of my entrepreneurial progress and admired that I was young and in business for myself. As a result, he asked if I was interested in becoming a church trustee. I gladly took the position and was exposed to the inner workings of the church administration. The church, at this time, had 450 to 500 active members, and I was tasked, along with nine other people, to handle the counting and recording of the church money after each service.

Wisdom and Understanding Note

Never reject a position of elevation. There are many reasons why God will lay you on the heart of your leaders. There may very well be something that God wants to teach you. Working with the trustees and learning how important tasks were carried out taught me the right way to do things, as well as what never to do. If you try it out and decide that it's not for you or if the position is causing you to have another issue, you can always back out. The important thing is to follow the leading of God.

NO MORE SHACKING... LOL

During this period, I was still living at my parent's home with my fiancé. Although she lived upstairs while I lived in the basement, my pastor suggested that we should get married since we were living under the same roof. Melissa had also been tasked with being the youth director, and he thought that, as leaders in the church, it was better that we get married if we were going to live together. We were going to get married soon anyway, but I left it up to Melissa. To my surprise, she didn't have any problem with it at all. In fact, she was actually excited. So, we set the date and planned for a small, simple wedding at the church. I believed it was the right thing to do, and we both felt that we were honoring God in doing so. On July 30th, 1998, just over a year after our first meeting, we were married.

BABY NUMBER ONE ON THE WAY

In November 1998, my wife came home after a doctor's visit and told me she was expecting a baby. I really can't describe the feeling I had when she told me the news. I do remember thinking that life just changed for me in so many ways. *A Baby! Wow, Allen, you will be a dad soon.* This thought stayed in my head until my baby boy was born. *Elijah!*

This new development made me want to step up as a man more than ever. I started to imagine all the things I could do with my new baby. Of course, I didn't know if it was going to be a girl or a boy, but I was excited for whatever. Sometimes, I would question myself as to whether I was ready to raise a child. Then I would dismiss the thoughts and conclude that if I was doing the right thing and keeping God in my life, I would be okay.

PURCHASING OUR FIRST HOME

In February 1999, we closed the deal on our first home. Prior to the wedding, we had started saving money. Instead of spending the money we had saved on a big wedding like we had planned, we were now focused on buying our first house together. We were able to save about $30,000 in one year by working together and putting away $2000 - 3000 a month in savings. The barbershop we opened together was doing extremely well. I had decided to close the first shop a few months before because my brother had gone on to open his own barbershop. It made sense to downsize to one shop. This turned out to be a great business move. It also gave my wife time to be with our newborn in our new home.

MINISTRY GROWING PAINS

Approximately nine months into working in the ministry, I began to have slight disagreements with my pastor. He wanted me to follow his format and style of preaching. He wanted everyone in the class to write their sermons down, and then preach them word for word by reciting what was on the paper. I didn't see this as the best way for me to preach a sermon. I wanted to preach from my heart with a few main points put together in an outline. I didn't want to be dependent or confined to a piece of paper if the spirit led me to say something else or elaborate on a specific point or topic. However, he made it clear to me that I needed to write my sermons down word for word. Now let me say that I enjoyed it when my pastor preached. His style was highly effective in the way he wrote down his sermons and read it to the congregation. I just didn't feel it was going to be equally effective for me to use his method of preaching. Besides, in my dream, I was not preaching the way he was trying to make me do it.

> ### Wisdom and Understanding Note
>
> I know that in many traditional church settings, you cannot disagree with the pastor. I felt that I was protecting my gifts and my development of the gift to speak without a piece of paper in front of me. As a Pastor myself, I think it's important to get an assessment of everyone. If God called that person to a specific area of ministry, I would make necessary corrections as they are growing to help aid their gift. As a leader, I would never teach anyone to do anything exactly as I do it. This is what I felt was going to be a problem for me.

Sometime had gone by and I was beginning to get the hang of ministry knowledge. My disagreement with my pastor was, however, slowing things down. Everybody was doing what he asked and preaching their sermons word for word, but I insisted that I couldn't do it that way. In one Wednesday night service, everyone in the ministry class was required to preach a 10-minute sermonette. The Pastor asked us to write our sermons down and preach them, but he didn't analyze our sermon prior to us presenting them as he promised he would. Unlike most of my colleagues who wrote down their sermons word for word, I wrote down three points from the scriptures I was using, but I planned to speak from my heart.

After the service, two of the church's deacons (coincidentally, they were both named deacon Michael) came up to me and asked if I had written my sermon down. I told them that I hadn't. They told me that they were moved by the sermon. I had noticed this from the reaction of the church in general. This was the style I wanted to stick to and what I believed God was leading me to do. I began sharing this perspective of mine with my pastor but unfortunately, that was when our issues started getting worse.

Based on my not being able to adapt to his format of preaching and a few other things, he called a minister meeting out of the blue. I had a funny feeling that this meeting would be about me. I didn't want to be out of order, so I attended the meeting. At the start of the meeting, the pastor began speaking on things entirely unrelated to the issue at hand. As the meeting proceeded, I began to sense that the topic was edging closer to me. After he reiterated that being part of the ministry class required following orders, he opened the floor to the other ministers to respond to a question: "What does it mean to be insubordinate?" The ministers went around the room and defined in their own words, what they thought it meant to be insubordinate. It just so happened that I was the last person to respond. The entire time the others were responding, I was thinking that I couldn't believe a meeting was called for such a thing. I thought to myself, *Why not pull me to the side and discuss with me what you felt?* Nevertheless, what I had sensed in my spirit was confirmed at this point.

When it was my turn to speak, the first thing I said was, "It's obvious that this 'random' meeting was called for me." I made it clear that I wasn't in 100 percent agreement with some of the things the leadership wanted. I said, in the nicest way possible, that I thought it was wrong for everyone to be a carbon copy, and that we all had giftings that should be enhanced and nurtured accordingly. I further stated that it wasn't that I didn't want to follow leadership, but I felt that I couldn't do things exactly the way the pastor did it. I would only be a copy of him, which would stunt my growth and not allow me to do things the way God was showing me. I spoke from my heart and waited to see their response. That was where it all turned left.

The pastor's wife said, "If you don't want to be here, you don't have to be here." I was shocked. I had intentionally spoken as gently as I could as I made my points. I hadn't meant to offend anyone, but apparently, I had. Everyone in the room was extremely quiet. After I recovered from the shock of what had just happened, I stood up and said, "Sorry" to everyone, shook the hands of the two younger elders sitting next to me, and headed to the door. I wished everyone a blessed night and made my exit.

Walking to my car, I began to wonder about the decision I made. *Did I make the right decision? Would I have to start all over somewhere else? Was God mad at me for excusing myself from the church?* A host of other thoughts followed. I had already dedicated almost a year of my life to this ministry, and I knew leaving meant that I had to start all over again. I silently prayed and asked God if I had done the right thing, and then I got into my car and drove off. The next morning, I woke up to a call from the pastor. I was expecting him to lash out at me or vent his displeasure and anger, but to my surprise, that wasn't the case. He said, "Allen, I respect what you did yesterday at the meeting. You believed in what you believed in and you stood for it." But he didn't say anything about me coming to the church. I made up my mind that I was going to stick to my decision. I no longer wanted the tension we had to affect the learning and growth I desired as a young minister.

Sometimes, great things can come out of conflict. The irony of it all is that we all became closer after this event and remained cordial in our future dealings. What's amazing is how God used Bishop Lester Williams later in my journey to get this book out. I will share exactly how later.

Wisdom and Understanding Note

Where you start may not always be where you finish. That church was where I first saw the light. However, the tension provoked the change I needed to move on and be replanted. God knows exactly what you need to develop you. It's not the end of the road when disagreements come. It may only mean that He is going to replant you somewhere else to grow. Always learn from previous conflicts and move on as a better person.

FINDING A NEW CHURCH

The next day at the barbershop, I was cutting my client, Tim. We were having a conversation about God which I often did. I can't really remember what we were discussing, but I do remember that he started talking about his mother starting a new church. Because of what I had just gone through, my interest was piqued. I told Tim, my customer, that I was in the process of looking for a new church home. I gave him my number and told him to give it to his mother so we could talk. The next day after, we spoke on the phone.

The conversation we had was mostly about our respective histories and current journeys in the ministry. I discovered that she had completed seminary school and had experienced a host of other things in the ministry. We also discussed where I was at with the learning and teaching I was receiving at my previous church, and the seminary college I was attending. One of the things my church had encouraged in the ministry program was to enroll in seminary if you were able to afford it. So, that is what I had done under the direction of my first pastor. I shared all this with Tim's mother in our first conversation. We had a great talk, which helped me to lean towards visiting her church. I discussed it with my wife, and she was pretty much in agreement with whatever decision I thought we should make. The following Sunday, my wife and I made plans to attend this new church.

When we arrived at the church, Tim's mother, another woman who was a minister, and one other lady were the only ones in attendance. My previous church had over 400 regular attenders, so this was different. All things must start from somewhere, so I was glad to help grow the new church. The service began as she played worship and praise songs from a cd player. Again, this was different, but I was perfectly fine with it because we sang unto the Lord.

The service went on as a normal program, and then it was time for God's Word to be brought forth. As she spoke, I was getting a lot from what she was saying, and I was into her delivery. She spoke in a medium level tone and with a consistent flow. I thought *I could receive her teaching style.* By the end of her preaching, I felt that God had used her to speak to my heart. She opened the doors to join the church, and I stood up to accept the invitation. I didn't know it at the time, but my wife wasn't too happy with my decision. She agreed to go to the church but hadn't decided if she wanted to be there as a member. I had to apologize, and I promised her that I would at least consult with her before I did something like that again. Nevertheless, we now had a new church home.

The following Sunday, as we prepared to visit our new church home, I was excited. I felt like it was a new beginning for me to learn and serve the Lord. When we arrived, it was the same as the previous week. We sang worship and praise songs for 10-15 minutes, and then the pastor opened with a morning scripture and prayer. After a few announcements and one more congregational song, the pastor began to preach. Unlike the previous week, she began to scream at us and speak God's wrath on us! I didn't know what to think. I did know that I had a different feeling than I had during the message the week before.

This became the ongoing theme, week after week. It was never again like the first time we attended. However, I'm the type of person who doesn't give up too easily. After a few months had gone by, I asked her if she would like me to help or assist in any area of the ministry. Her response revealed why there are so many denominational beliefs, even though we all read the same Bible. Her answer for not letting me help in the church after being there for two months kind of blew me away. She had not asked me to participate because, as she put it, "You are not SAVED!"

CHAPTER 8

YES, I AM SAVED!

I believe going to this new church was part of God's way of building me up and exposing me more in ministry. It exposed me to the different beliefs of the different denominations in the Christian faith--and there are a lot of them. Even though all Christian denominations believe in Jesus, there are scriptural or doctrinal differences that make each one unique in its beliefs.

When I got to this new church, the pastor knew that I was in ministry training and theology school because we had a discussion on the matter. After I had been attending her church for a few months, I asked her why I was not being used to help in any area of the ministry. She responded, "Because you are not **SAVED**!" She continued by saying that the only thing that would convince her that I was saved was if I spoke in tongues in front of her. I was confused because I had already received the baptism of the Holy Spirit while at my previous church. I asked her why she believed that I wasn't saved, even though I had told her all of my history. She said that she had never *seen* me praying in tongues. I explained that, if she was expecting to see me praying in tongues in front of her to prove my salvation, then she would probably never see me do it.

This discussion with the pastor caused me to start researching the scriptures more. I found later that, in the book of Acts, there were thirteen occasions where people were saved (converted). In two cases, there is evidence of speaking in tongues immediately after being saved. As I began to see these things, I realized that this was one of the differences between many denominations. This was a case of how people had different understandings of what made a person truly saved, and how and when the Holy Spirit began residing in the heart of that person.

After a few weeks of going back and forth, the pastor invited me to a meeting with her bishop, and I accepted the offer. It was obvious to me that she must have been talking to the bishop about my salvation, so I wanted to know what that was all about. After a Sunday service, we went to see the bishop. The bishop's church was about three miles down the road from our church. When we entered, he was still preaching. I was standing on the side when he called me to come up front.

I can't remember everything the bishop said, but I know he laid his hands on me and started praying that I receive the baptism of the Holy Spirit. I was surprised because I knew I had already received the baptism of the Holy Spirit and that I had prayed in tongues in my previous church, but because I didn't want to be in disagreement with the bishop, I began to pray in agreement with him. Soon, I felt so overwhelmed with the Spirit that I began praying in tongues. I prayed so long in tongues that even when I wanted to stop and start speaking English, I couldn't. The congregation began to clap and started saying that I got saved. This was another surprise to me. I knew that I was already saved and had many interactions with the Lord before this encounter and that I was already praying in tongues. This didn't feel right to me. This church clearly had a serious doctrinal issue, as far as I was concerned. That was the last day I attended that church. I didn't want to tell people that they were not saved because they didn't speak in tongues. I knew that I would have a problem teaching that doctrinal belief, so I removed myself from this church and concluded that I'd have to start over again.

Wisdom and Understanding Note

When I gave my life to Christ, I must be honest: I thought it would be smooth sailing. He showed me what I would be doing, and I thought the road was going to be smooth. That shows how little I understood God's process.

Sometimes the route that God will put you on is not a clear path from point A to point B. In this chapter, you see that there were differences of opinion which brought conflict and resistance. Looking back, I see that God put obstacles in my path so that I could learn. I wouldn't have learned about deep denominational issues and how they separate the church if I hadn't gone through this process.

God has His way of building your faith to trust Him. He doesn't want you to rely on a man. Some Christians feel that they are not in a position to question authority in the church when they feel something is not right. I would suggest that you simply ask to get understanding.

NO MISTAKES WITH GOD

After this point, I began praying again and seeking God as to where to start over from. My wife suggested that we take our time moving forward, and I agreed. So, we visited several different churches over the next year. During this time, there was an addition added to the family. My second baby boy. *Isaiah!*

I can't remember why, but we decided to visit my parent's church in mid-2001. My parent's church was a larger church with over 200 members at the time. The church was pastored by Pastor Lemon Johnson. As we walked into the church, she noticed me and signaled for me to come to sit upfront with the ministers. I didn't want to create a distraction by declining, so I went to the pulpit to take a seat. I believed that she was mistaken. I knew that only ordained or lay ministers should sit in the pulpit during service. Since she called me up there, she must have thought I was one or the other.

After the service, I asked if I could speak to her for a moment. She agreed but wanted to meet in her office after she said goodbye to a few people. Sitting in the comfort of her office, I asked her why she had called me up to the pulpit to sit with the other ministers. I wasn't ordained or even a lay minister. She told me that my mother had shared that I was in training as a minister at my church. She was under the assumption that, since it had been a few years since then, I must already be a minister. Then God showed me that His timing was exactly perfect.

GOD KEEPS ME ON SCHEDULE

As soon as I told Pastor Johnson that I was yet to be licensed and that I didn't even have a church home at the time, she said my family could remain and serve at New Covenant Church of Christ. Further, she told me that she was going to set me up for a trial sermon the following Wednesday, and that she would have the congregation there. Afterward, they would vote as to whether they believed that I expressed the witness of preaching, and if I was called to the ministry. After she said this, I was wowed. The reason for my "wow" experience was because I would have been a licensed minister right about that same time Pastor Johnson was planning to set up the trial sermon if I had stayed in the first church. God was showing me to build trust in Him and His timing, as well as everything else He had shown me. I had thought that those things were slipping out of my hands, but here was God, showing me things were right on time.

Wisdom and Understanding Note

If there is one thing I would want you to get here, it is that God will allow someone to see something in you that you don't see in order to put you right in the place where He wants you to be.

Pastor Johnson had me do that first sermon, and I will never forget it. The first sermon I preached was entitled, "Don't worry. God's got you." It was a Wednesday night, and there were about 70 people in attendance. My foundational text for that night was Matthew 6:26, about how God made man understand that if the birds didn't need to sow or reap, neither store in barns, then we didn't need to worry because we had much more value to Him as humans.

There was a girl in the service named Wednesday Knight who was a friend of mine from childhood. We used to play together any time I visited my mother's church when I was younger. This young lady was suffering from multiple sclerosis at a very tender age, and it was so bad that she couldn't walk without crutches or support. She was sitting in the audience that night as I preached. At the end of the sermon, the pastor asked people in the audience to stand up if they believed God had called me to preach, and if they could bear witness to it. Wednesday Knight was the first person to stand up, without her crutches or support of any kind. She was standing straight up even before the pastor could finish her sentence, and there was this big smile on her face that will forever be etched in my memory. Everyone in that room stood up that night and attested to the fact that there was no question I was called of God to minister His Word.

I had thought that I would have to start all over after I left my first church, but here I was, two years later, standing and getting licensed to become a minister, true to God's plan and promise.

Wisdom and Understanding Note

When you submit your will to God's will, everything will go according to His plan.

CHAPTER 9

GET OUT OF YOUR COMFORT ZONE

As I continued to walk with God, I was taking note of all the things He was doing for me. Some small and some big, but I was truly convinced that it was God who was making all things possible for me. I started to hear God's voice more as I began to trust Him deeper. I actually believe I heard Him more because I desired for Him to speak to me more.

As I was serving actively in the ministry at the New Covenant Church of Christ, I was beginning to grow more in my Christian walk and in my ministry. I was beginning to trust more in God and was starting to allow myself to be led, more and more, by His Spirit.

I was invited to an ordination service at my cousin's church in New Jersey. I lived in New York at this time, which meant that I had to travel for about two hours to get to this church for the service. I took $180 with me but didn't take any credit or debit cards with me. I didn't use credit cards at that time, and I didn't keep debit cards on me so as not to spend unnecessary money. We spent $40 on gas and a few snacks before arriving at the service.

As the ceremony was ending, the church set up to take an offering. I had intended to drop $100 into the offering basket. As the basket was coming my way, I heard a voice (Holy Spirit) whisper that I should put all the money in my pocket in the offering. That didn't make any sense to me, being a logical person. I wondered how I was going to get home if I heeded the voice. I couldn't trust that my wife would have money on her either because most of the time, I usually held enough money for both of us. So, this was a dilemma for me.

I decided to give only the $100, as I had planned. After the ushers had stopped passing around the baskets, the Spirit was still telling me to go drop the remaining $40 in my pocket into the offering basket. Of course, I argued once again because I had already calculated, in my head, what was needed to get back home to New York. I knew I had to get home through a route that required me to pay three different toll gates before I could get home – the New Jersey Turnpike, the George Washington Bridge, and the Throgs Neck Bridge. Because of this, I held on to that $40, which I kept tucked away in my back pocket.

As I left the church, deep down I felt like I did something wrong. I sat in my car outside the church just thinking to myself that maybe I should have listened to the voice that kept speaking to me. For some reason, I didn't share the ordeal with my wife. I think deep down, I was embarrassed to tell her I did not listen to the Holy Spirit. I didn't know what she would have said. So, I just decided to keep it to myself.

We headed back to New York. As I drove, I was thinking about the instructions I didn't listen to at the church. We had been driving for about 20 minutes, and the toll gate for the New Jersey

Turnpike was about a mile away. I was thinking to myself that all I needed to do was reach into my back pocket and get the $40 to cover the fee for the first toll. About that time, my wife turned to me and said, "Babe, I have $40 that I brought from home. Do you need it?" At that moment, I felt so stupid. I began to wonder why in the world I had chosen not to listen to the instruction from God.

LEARN TO TRUST GOD'S INSTRUCTIONS

The lesson I learned from this was not about the amount of money or putting it all in the basket. The lesson was more about the fact that I didn't trust the voice of God when it was noticeably clear to me. God was literally saying, "Don't worry. I am going to get you home," but I didn't listen to Him. I felt so bad. This event was the beginning of me trusting God more with my finances. Prior to this event, God would ask me to do things, but none of them required me having to trust Him totally. The rest of the way home, I couldn't believe that my wife had the money in her pocket the whole time, and all I needed to do was just trust God. This is one story about God increasing my faith that I will forever cherish.

Wisdom and Understanding Note

Learning to hear the voice of God is extremely essential if you are going to make progress with Him. Many people think that God only speaks through stories or instruction in the Bible. That is just one aspect of how God can deliver to you, very important instructions. The next time you hear the Holy Spirit nudging you to do something that doesn't make any logical sense, act in faith

> to see what the outcome will be. In doing so, you will learn how to identify when it is truly the Holy Spirit talking to you.

BOUND BY TRADITION

I had spent some time serving at the New Covenant Church of Christ. Pastor Johnson shared with me that I could serve there until I found a church home. Soon, my wife and I started looking for a place to call home. We couldn't really go along with so much of the tradition that was in the church, though I loved the people there. We wanted to grow, and it seemed impossible to do it there.

Serving as a minister there, I would often speak with the other ministers who had been there before me. I soon discovered that the pastor had no intention of ordaining anyone. It didn't matter how long you were there, the tradition at this church was to not ordain any minister. I also discovered that other ministers had left the ministry--in good standing--to start their own churches, but the pastor would not ordain them for their new assignment. Even though I was grateful that she acknowledged my call to ministry and licensed me as a minister, I began to think it was pointless to remain there. I had learned how to visit the sick, improved in my preaching, and carried out other duties as a minister, but now I felt it was time to move on. I decided to confirm a few things with the pastor before I made my departure.

I set up a meeting with Pastor Johnson and asked her about my ordination status. I wanted to know if there were any plans to prepare me for that level of ministry. From her response, it seemed that was off the table in this church. All that I had heard others tell me was 100% confirmed. This was obviously discouraging to me, and I eventually stopped attending services.

The pastor asked my father about me, and he came to see me. I remember my father's words vividly. He said, "You shouldn't leave the church because they would give you a letter as a reference to where you are going next." I had made up my mind and wasn't concerned about a reference letter. I also had the mindset that I didn't need a letter from anywhere. I had seen the Lord move in His own timing. I was pretty much done and had no interest in developing or moving forward in a church where there was no room to grow.

THE HOLY SPIRIT WILL CONVICT YOU WHEN YOU ARE WRONG

God is a God of order, and when you are wrong, the Holy Spirit will show you. Later, when I thought about how I had left the church, the Holy Spirit showed me that I had been wrong. I was wrong for leaving without giving the pastor a notice of my departure. God didn't let this behavior of mine fly. I had to fix my wrong and make it right.

Wisdom and Understanding Note

Even though you could be 100% right in your convictions, you must conduct yourself in decency and in order. If you are a child of God, then that is the way He would want you to conduct yourself in all your affairs. If you don't, you are sowing negative seeds that will come back to you one way or another.

PRAYING FOR A MAJOR CHANGE IN MY LIFE

In mid-2002, I had only one barbershop, and it was running smoothly. It was around this time that I started to feel I wasn't spending enough time with my family. I was always terribly busy, spending long days at the shop. One day, my wife went out with my sister-in-law, Kimmy, and they took some pictures with the kids. When I saw those pictures, I stared at them for a long time. Something was wrong with them. Then I had a revelation.

While staring at the pictures, I noticed that I wasn't in them. I felt so pressed that I was missing opportunities to spend time with my young family. This began to stress me out and led me to pray a kind of prayer that I wouldn't normally pray. I asked God for some particular changes in my life. I told Him I wanted to do different things, and I wanted more time with my wife and two kids. I also had a few other projects I was working on and desired for these projects to take off. If they did, I wouldn't need the barbershop income and could provide for my family with new ventures.

When God responded to this prayer, He told me that if I wanted the freedom and the time I so desired, I needed to get rid of the barbershop and my house and start all over with Him leading me. I would basically have to trust Him 100% and jump out the window.

At this time, I had a point of reference as to what God could do. I knew He spoke to me and, as a result, He showed me who He was, but when I received the answer from this prayer, I was not "all the way there" in faith.

Up until this point in my life, I had always worked for myself and relied on myself. To put all my trust in God and let Him make it happen for me on another level was not going to be easy. There were times, after I heard this instruction, that I questioned if I had heard the right thing. So, I decided to get involved in a new business to see if I could keep my income flowing from the barbershop while I tried something new at the same time. The result of this was that I ventured into the mortgage business. I was basically processing mortgage loans to help people get financing for their homes. I learned the whole business while working with an attorney I knew, but the irony was that, after four months, I was yet to make much money from all my endeavors. I had to end that venture and go back full time to the barbershop. When I prayed about it again, God gave the same answer as the first time. He wanted me to get rid of the house and the barbershop, and start all over from scratch, completely trusting in Him alone! I wasn't supposed to try to keep the barbershop at all.

> **Wisdom and Understanding Note**
>
> When you get instructions from God, you must do exactly what He is instructing. If you try to justify another way of doing what God called you to do by adding your own twist, you will most likely fail and waste time in getting where He wants you to be.

When I realized that this wasn't going to change, I put my barbershop up for sale. I ended up finding a buyer for it right about the same time I found one for the house. I had purchased my house in 1999 for $152,000, and I sold it for $304,000. After I took care of some essential bills and a second mortgage, I was left with around $100,000. I also sold the barbershop for $42,000 for which I received $21,000 in cash and the remaining $21,000 in a promissory note.

Prior to my selling both shops, my wife and I had traveled to Virginia to see how we felt about moving there and starting all over. We loved it and had our minds set on moving to Virginia. After we sold the house, however, we visited Virginia again and didn't love it at all. The feelings we had earlier had completely left us, and we were clueless as to what we should do next.

Our home was sold, and we had less than a month to leave. Not having a plan, I asked my parents if we could stay with them for a couple of weeks. So, with no plans and just a good amount of money, we moved in with my parents with the intention of staying no longer than a month. My plan was to seek God for some clarity on where we should move. Well, God did start speaking with me, but it really wasn't what I was looking to hear. God had other plans.

PHASE THREE

Life Trusting Jesus Christ

CHAPTER 10

GOD ARE YOU SERIOUS?

I was ready for this new chapter in my life to begin. The house was sold, and it was the first time since I was fourteen that I would be completely putting the clippers down to generate income. I wasn't 100 percent sure as to how I was going to make a living, but I was believing and trusting God to make a way for me.

Before the move to my parent's house, my wife shared with me that she was pregnant with our third child. I wasn't scared, but I knew that I had to get things to provide for us all. Every day, I would wake up and ask God what He wanted me to do. I had all the money from the sale of my house and barbershop, and I just wanted to know the next line of action. When God finally responded to my prayers, He instructed me to give all my money away from the sale of the barbershop and house. I immediately dismissed it and started making up excuses as to why I believed that it wasn't God who was talking to me at this time. I thought I was yet to hear from Him correctly.

REMEMBER - GOD CAN SPEAK IN MORE WAYS THAN ONE

On regular occasions, while in my parent's house, I would turn on the cable to the Word Network. I listened to testimonies from many preachers and individuals. It had to be God's timing because each time, it seemed that the testimonies were about how someone gave a large sum of money away, even to their last dollar. Then how God had blessed them greatly for exercising their faith. I heard this type of thing on several occasions. Sometimes I would just turn off the TV so as to not hear testimonies about giving money away. Miraculously, even after staying off the Word Network for a week, I would turn the TV back on, only to hear yet another story of this kind. At this point, I was still doubting if this was what God wanted me to do, but I couldn't shake the feeling that it was.

Wisdom and Understanding

Pay attention to what you keep seeing and hearing over and over. God has a way to provide what you need to hear in each season, based on the instruction He has for you to follow. It's amazing when He does it. You become aware of it, and then you follow it. Once you respond to Him and carry out the task, it stops!

SOWING MY FIRST BIG SEED

I began seeking God more on this issue and, as I prayed, I felt God was leading me to sow a big seed. While I was praying, God showed me my first pastor, Bishop Williams, who I had had a disagreement with. I felt God leading me to give him some money; so I gave Bishop Williams a call. I booked an appointment with him and headed over to his office. As I sat parked in my car, I was trying to write a $7000 check, but I felt God telling me to write $8000 instead. After attempting to write $7000 a few more times, I just yielded to the Holy Spirit and finally wrote the $8000 check. I then exited my car and went into his office to speak with him.

After our chat and a brief prayer, I folded the check so he couldn't see the amount written on it, and I handed it over to him. I told him the amount of money was a seed laid on my heart to give to him and that he was free to use the money any way he would like. He took the check from me but didn't look at it as I left. Later that night, Bishop Williams gave me a call and told me that the $8000 was exactly the amount he needed for his current situations. God knew exactly what was going on when He prompted me to write that check.

God had me change the seven to number eight for a reason. It kept bugging me, so I went to the Christian bookstore to find a book on numbers. I discovered that the number eight represents new beginnings. What I took from it was God telling me He would do a new thing with me. This $8000 was the biggest seed I had given to anyone in my life up to that point, and I thought that, because I had given this seed, God would make things start to happen right away.

I prayed that God would help me sell products and help me get new business opportunities and ideas going. I was hoping that God would do all this immediately because of this seed I had given, but I was wrong. A few months passed and nothing happened. I kept praying and asking God when He would do it, but He didn't respond.

SPECIFICALLY TWO THINGS I WAS PRAYING FOR

Before I sold my house in 2003, there were two things I was trying to do. The first was an audio recording I did call 'The Legal Hustling Series'. I had wanted to start selling them all over the world, and of course, make money doing so. The second thing I had prayed about was trying to develop a website to start making money online. Before I sold the shop and my house, I had been working on these two things with no success at all.

PRAYER#1 - THE LEGAL HUSTLING SERIES

In late 2001, I created something I called 'The Legal Hustling Series'. How this came to be was my cousin, who was about thirteen, came to my house to speak with me. He told me he was thinking about selling drugs. This took me completely by surprise. I began telling him how my brother and I never had to take that route because we did other things to make money. I shared the things we had done to make legitimate money as we grew up: shoveling snow, cutting lawns, cutting hair, cleaning floors, and opening the booting company. I asked him why he would even consider selling drugs. He had seen what we did and could do the same things or similar to make money. I tried my best to discourage him from going the drug route. I was mad at him, and I let him know it but was also glad he came to talk with me about it.

When the conversation ended and he left, I was hurt by the way he was thinking. I wondered why he would even have those thoughts in the first place. I began thinking about how I could help him with the information I had learned over the years. Most of the information I had, at that time, was from my experience in business and from reading a lot of business and motivational books. I knew my cousin wasn't going to take the time to read all the literature, so I started thinking about how I could get him that kind of information.

After giving it a lot of thought, I had a new idea. I decided to record a 60-minute audio CD and give it to him so that he could study and learn without reading. I wanted him to understand that the things it took to run an illegal business were the same things you would do to set up a legal business. It took me about one week to lay out all that should be discussed on this audio. Once I had the outline ready, it was time for me to set up some studio time, and that is exactly what I did.

I went to the studio to record. The following day, the studio engineer added some background music to my vocals. This later turned out to be beneficial (I'll tell you why later). The audio was mixed and mastered, and I called it "The Legal Husting Series: Volume One." I began making some sales from the CDs when a couple of people began buying them in my barbershop. The truth is I made money, but it wasn't a lot to brag about. I knew the audio had great potential because of the feedback I was getting, but I really didn't know how to market them, plus the time I spent at the barbershop really didn't give me the time I needed to get them out there.

SELLING MY FIRST PRODUCT ON THE INTERNET

The internet in 2001 was very new to me. I put together a website to sell my Legal Hustling CD's but had extremely limited success. I got sales from direct marketing but just enough to break even for the ads I ran. So, it was at that point in 2001 that I stopped pushing the CD's.

PRAYER #2 BIG DREAMS FOR THE INTERNET

The internet was becoming bigger and bigger in the early 2000's. While learning a lot when building my first website in 2001, I started to discover the power of it. I was hooked on the fact that money was being made in a variety of ways online. It became my new fascination the more and more I sat in front of my computer. I soon discovered that I was limited in the skills necessary to do what I saw others doing on the internet, so I started seeking out help.

My friend, Dasul, was someone that I would often talk to about the internet. I asked him if he knew of anyone that could program websites. He said, "Yes" and introduced me to a guy named Carl in Brooklyn. I set up a meeting at his house to see if he could design a website for me.

Carl explained that he knew how to do web development and web design. I thought that was great since I wanted to do something bigger than what I had done with my previous work on my site. I hired him, and we began to work on some stuff. It wasn't long before I realized that, even though he had much better equipment and software than I did, he didn't really know that much. This was frustrating, and the work I was attempting to do never happened. I ended the project with him.

As I was looking for someone else to work with me, someone who happened to like my Legal Hustling CD's contacted me to give his testimony. This guy loved the recordings, and I ended up doing an interview with him. After the interview, we spoke a little more. He told me that he knew a guy who did web development and could work to enhance my current website. This is how I met a programmer named Jeff, who lived in Fort Greene projects in Brooklyn.

Jeff had been programming for some time when I met him. He was a lot more knowledgeable than Carl had been. I visited his place, and he helped me upgrade my website. In watching him, I started to discover more about how the backend of a website really worked. I learned exactly what was involved in building an interactive website.

Wisdom and Understanding Note

Any time I hire someone, I always take it as an opportunity to learn. Not because I want to do things on my own, but it's an opportunity to learn so that the next person doesn't try to get over on you.

After a few weeks of working and learning things from Jeff, he had moved out of the projects and into a new one-bedroom apartment near Coney Island. I went to visit him and met his girlfriend, Cindy, who was about five months pregnant. It was a nice apartment, but it was empty. Jeff just had a bed and a television in the bedroom, along with a table for his computer.

As I stood in the middle of his living room floor, God spoke clearly to me to give Jeff the furniture from my house, which I had in storage. I told them what God had just spoken to me, and they were excited. Jeff and Cindy were very thankful because it was something they weren't expecting at all. I paid for the U-Haul truck, and we went to grab the furniture. The next day, they invited their family and friends over to a house full of furniture and other things we blessed them with. They were extremely grateful, and I was so happy to see them happy.

Even though the Lord wasn't showing me the increase I wanted to see in my business, He was sending instructions like this for me to be a blessing to others. In no way was I worried, but I would often wonder how God was going to bless me for giving all my stuff away.

"Give, and it will be given to you: good measure, pressed down, shaken together, and running over will be put into your bosom. For with the same measure that you use, it will be measured back to you." Luke 6:38 NKJV

CHAPTER 11

LISTENING TO GOD'S DETAILED INSTRUCTIONS

In May 2003, while we were still living at my parent's house, my third child was born. *Josiah!* What a blessing it was to see this child delivered and be completely healthy! When my wife was about three months pregnant with him, the doctor saw a lump in one of his lungs, which had started to grow like a tumor. The doctor was alarmed, so he instructed my wife to continue to be seen. When she went for her check-up at the six-month mark, the tumor had grown bigger. We were continuously praying and believing God to remove the tumor. In the seventh month when we went to our third sonogram visit, the nurse couldn't find the lump or any sign of the tumor. She called the doctor into the room; he also checked my wife and didn't see the tumor. He looked through her chart to make sure they were looking in the right location and proceeded to look once again. No tumor! This was a miracle for us, as well as for the doctor and nurses in the room. God had intervened and my third child was born completely healthy and strong.

I had not imagined that I would be living at my parent's home with three kids and my wife. I was really trying desperately to get one of the businesses going before his arrival. We had been living with my parents for over four months, and now we were adding a newborn to the mix! I was beyond frustrated.

WAITING ON GOD AT MY PARENT'S HOUSE

Still waiting on instruction from the Lord, I decided to add volumes 2 and 3 to the Legal Hustling CD series. I basically recorded two more hours of the same helpful content and now had a three-CD set consisting of almost three hours of business information, and ways to make money. This time, I produced the music on volumes 2 and 3 myself. My friend, Greg, gave me a program called Reasons, from a company named Propellahead, and I made about 20 beats in three days. I paid to have the CDs professionally packaged and started marketing them. I was selling a few but didn't see the big explosion in sales that I desired. I had spent about $6,000 putting it all together, another $2000 setting up and selling at small business events, and about $3000 running ads in industry publications. I didn't really see too much success with the sales. At that time, I didn't really know how to market my own products, so I started looking for a professional who could possibly help me market the series. I didn't really have too much success finding anyone, so I started taking online marketing courses to learn how to effectively market and sell my products.

LEGAL HUSTLING SERIES

VOLUME 1 ORIGINALLY RELEASED IN 2001
VOLUME 2 AND 3 ORIGINALLY RELEASED IN 2003

Wisdom and Understanding Note

When you have a challenge and you can't seem to get the help you need, it may be God telling you to learn a new skill. It doesn't mean you will always need to use your own skills. However, knowing the skills you need will allow you to go further when you are left to get things done on your own.

I was still praying but not getting too much feedback from God. The Legal Hustling series and the web development didn't seem to be enough for me to feel confident moving out of my parent's house just yet. I thought at the time that, if I moved my family into our own place, we would end up losing it and have to move back to my parent's house. The only other way was to go back to cutting hair, which I couldn't do because it was exactly what I had prayed to be removed from. I had a direct instruction from God to not go back to cutting hair, which I will explain more later.

A few months after my son's birth, my wife and I decided we needed to get out of my parent's house for a while. We drove to Dallas, Texas to visit the Potter's House which is pastored by Bishop T.D. Jakes. We headed to Atlanta, Georgia first where my wife's best friend lived. We also visited a few churches there as well. Based on the leading of the Holy Spirit, we planted big financial seeds in every church we attended. This was how I kept sowing seed and giving money away according to detailed instructions from the Lord. When we reached Dallas, Texas, I was so amazed at the Potter's House and how God was using T.D. Jakes. He had basically mentored me from afar with many of his sermons. Prior to visiting his church, I had heard his testimony, which encouraged me to trust God even more with my giving.

Bishop Jakes and his wife decided to step out on faith and put their last savings into a book that he wanted to publish, so they stepped out on faith and believed God. The book sold millions of copies. It was that story, and many other testimonies, that encouraged me to keep giving. I was led to sow first, a $3000 seed, and then a $1000 seed in Potter's House Ministries.

MY MONEY IS GETTING LOW

Before this trip, my wife and I had decided to purchase a reliable vehicle, so we spent about $6500 on a minivan for the family. During the trip, we spent a lot of money and had lots of fun with our boys. Money was getting low, but I was still trusting God for a business breakthrough. Besides, we were enjoying ourselves as we traveled on this long road trip. It was a much needed time with my family. After visiting family in the south and a few other states, we made it back home around the end of August 2003.

By September 2003, God still had not opened any doors for me. The *Legal Hustling Series* website was up and dedicated to the sales of the CDs, but none of this was looking promising in terms of good returns. I started thinking that I needed to see if I could get something else going so that we could leave my parents' house. I started to work on an idea that I had come up with just a few months before the family road trip.

MAYBE THIS IS THE BIG IDEA

Before I took the trip with my family to Texas, I had registered a domain name, GotNerds.com. The idea was to build a portal for people to find technical support from individuals who knew all about computers and web development. I believe this idea came to me as I was having difficulty finding web programmers to help me with my web development needs. Although I thought it was a great idea back in 2003, I was never able to completely launch the concept. While trying to build the website, I had learned how to code my own website from scratch, which basically gave me the skills I needed to develop a database-driven site.

I spent 14-16 hours a day working on Gotnerds.com. My father would leave for work at 6 am in the morning, and I would be in the same spot working when he came back home at 6 pm. I was trying my hardest to get the site launched. I bought books on programming and searched the web for information on web development. By this time, my money was getting low, and finding an affordable programmer would have completely depleted the remainder of my money. With all the traveling and the giving, my cash funds were now less than $10,000.

(Eventually, I sold the GotNerds.com domain in 2015 for $2500 to a couple of guys in Brooklyn. They wanted to launch a tech company. I wasn't using it and had no plans for it, so I decided to sell it.)

GOD, ARE YOU STILL HERE?

While I was still trying to make something happen, God was not giving me the much-needed feedback. I found myself at times overwhelmed with stress. The devil would often enter my thoughts around this time. I often wondered if I had done the right thing in giving so much money away. I thought about my kids' future and questioned if I had done the right thing for them. I saw my wife sleeping in a 12 x 14 bedroom with my kids and wondered again if I had done the right thing. The toughest part was having to listen to what some members of my family were saying: "What is Allen doing?" "Why does he have his wife and kids staying with his parents?" Word would get back to me and, as a man, I felt crushed. Although it got to me a lot, it didn't make me stop moving forward. I still had my faith in God and the process I believed in. But still, I sometimes wondered, "God, are You still there?"

TEMPTATION TO GO BACK TO THE BARBERSHOP

As I stayed in my parents' house and waited for God's promise and instructions, I had to keep busy. One of the things God had earlier told me in prayer was that I couldn't go back to cutting hair. I didn't understand this instruction initially, but I later realized that if I had gone back to cutting hair, I wouldn't have stayed committed to God's detailed instructions when the going got tough.

I learned a lot from not listening the first time when I was trying to step away from the barbershop. The fact that I kept it and didn't get rid of it gave me a crutch. When the going got tough, I would run back to it for safety, and God knew that I would. That's why I believe, to this day, that for the new things to produce in my life, I had to get rid of everything.

CHAPTER 12

BEFORE I FORMED THEE, I HAVE ORDAINED THEE

Sometime around September of 2003, I started to get confirmation from God about moving forward in ministry. I wasn't 100% sure what I was supposed to do, but I kept my spiritual ear open to see where God would lead me. I wasn't sure if I was supposed to start a church or maybe an outreach teaching ministry. I just knew in my spirit that God was preparing me to move forward. I had no objections to this but was concerned that I had not yet been ordained as a minister. I began to seek the Lord for direction pertaining to the next move.

As I prayed about being ordained, God shared with me that I needed to make things right with my first pastor, Bishop Lester Williams, and my parents' pastor, Reverend Lemon Johnson. I had left these two pastors on a sour note, and now I felt God telling me to go and smooth out the rough edges. Somewhere in the back of my mind, I imagined that, when I obeyed this instruction, the result would be one of the two pastors ordaining me.

I made an appointment with my first pastor, Bishop Williams. When I got to his place, I started by offering an apology for how things had happened in our past. After asking him to forgive me if I had ever offended him in any way, we continued to talk about things going on in the ministry. I shared with him that God was calling me to start something. He offered to help me with the condition that I would be starting where I had left off. In other words, I would be making up almost three years of studies under his leadership. He gave me four books to read and study and wanted me to start attending classes. I thought about it for a week and then let him know I would not be attending. I knew that God had told me to go to him to make amends, but I didn't believe that God wanted me to sit for almost three years to be ordained. I knew in my heart that God told me I was ready to move forward now, not three years from now. There was no bad blood at all, and he respected my decision when I withdrew. We continued to have a great relationship for many years after.

Shortly after this, I made an appointment with the pastor of my mother's church and on her invitation, I went to see her. I acknowledged that I was wrong and apologized to her for suddenly leaving the church without notice. I admitted that I should have given fair warning in the event that she would have needed to prepare for my absence, that it would have been the right thing to do. She accepted my apology, and we spoke briefly. I shared with her that I felt the Spirit was leading me to start a ministry. She acknowledged what I said and offered to help in any way she could. However, she didn't offer to prepare me for ordination even though she knew I wasn't ordained. I wasn't going to ask her because I felt that my ordination would be in line with God's plan. In His timing, someone would offer to ordain me, and then I would be free to accept.

I set up the two meetings as God had instructed me to do, and I had made amends. I had been almost 100% sure that one of those meetings would result in one of the pastors hearing what I had to say and then getting me immediately prepared for ordination. This was not the case. I went to God and asked the reason for going back to them, He clearly gave me an answer: I was getting ready to move forward in ministry, and I didn't need to have any bad blood that would hinder my progress. So, God inspired me to make all things right before He moved me forward.

Wisdom and Understanding Note

When possible, always go back to anyone you think you need to apologize to so that God can bless your forward movement. Many prayers and successes could be hindered when you don't make things right with your brothers and sisters in the body of Christ!

MOVING FORWARD WITH GOD'S PLAN

Even though I thought it was possible that one of the pastors would call me out the way God showed me, they didn't. As I sat in my mother's dining room, speaking to God about the fact that I was yet to be ordained, I was led by the Holy Spirit to move forward anyway and start preparing for ministry.

In the middle of October 2003, my wife and I started taking pictures to put on our ministry flyers and our website. I started looking for a place to conduct our first meeting. It was around November 2003 when I found a banquet hall that rented space for events. I thought it would be a good place to start, so I arranged to use the location once a week for $140 each time.

I was set to start this ministry in the first week of December. As I was sitting at my parents' dining room table, putting all the details together for marketing material, cards, the website, etc., my uncle, Bishop White, who lived in Texas called me out of the blue. I hadn't spoken to him in a few months, so I was a little surprised when he called. We started talking and, during the conversation, he asked me what I was doing. I told him I was starting my own ministry and putting some material together for promotion. He congratulated me and then asked me when I got ordained. I replied, "I haven't been ordained yet." His next response was, "I'm flying to New York to ordain you."

Our First Ministry Picture
November 2003
Pastor Allen and Melissa Brown

ONLY GOD CAN COORDINATE TIME LIKE THIS

While we were still on the call, I told my uncle that I didn't have a church building but that I was renting a banquet hall for my services. He said that was perfect and for me to think of a date for him to come. Right after he said that he told me to wait a minute while he looked at his calendar. So, I waited for a minute or two. He came back to the phone and asked me what I thought about February 7th, 2004. I told him I would have to check with the banquet hall to see if that date was available.

I called the hall and the lady I usually dealt with answered the phone. I told her I needed a date in February for an ordination service. She quickly responded that the hall was all booked up for February, and they had no dates available. I was a little crushed to hear her say that, but then, she asked me to hold on so she could do a double-check. I waited on hold for 2-3 minutes. When she returned to the line, she told me that the entire month of February was booked except for one date and time: February the 7th, 11 am to 2 pm was free. Only God could have set that up! She had been sure all the dates were taken in February; she had told me that practically before I had asked the question. For her to then come to the phone with the exact date that Bishop White had suggested was nothing less than the Holy Spirit doing what He does best. Not only was this a miraculous surprise, but it was also a confirmation that I was meant to be ordained that day. I called my uncle back immediately and shared the news with him, and then we concluded plans for him to fly to New York for the February 7th ordination service.

December came and I started conducting evening services. By this time, my wife and I were down to about $1200 in cash, though we still had the promissory note from the barbershop which was worth about $18,000. Our money was extremely low, but we were still believing God for the breakthrough.

ORDINATION DAY

On February 7, 2004, Bishop White arrived from Texas and officiated the ordination service where I became an ordained minister. The most amazing thing about it all was God's timing. I was getting ordained at the same time I would have if I stayed in my first church. Only God can make things work like that in our lives. I had no logical understanding at the time as to how God would do it all, but He did it all and kept me on time.

On that day, Bishop White preached from **Jeremiah 1:5 "Before I formed thee in the belly, I knew thee; and before thou camest forth out of the womb I sanctified thee, and I ordained thee a prophet unto the nations."**

Wisdom and Understanding Note

You can be assured that if you are following God, He will keep you on time with his schedule. The key thing is to make sure you are following Him.

NO MORE CASH!

We continued holding service until, eventually, we were all out of cash, and I could no longer pay to rent space at the hall. The members we had were young and didn't have the income to contribute to the rental space, so we had to stop the meetings. All the money I had made from the sale of the house was gone, and the only money we had left were the payments coming from the remaining balance on the promissory note from the barbershop sale. In all honesty, I felt like a failure and the devil started using those emotions against me.

With the ministry now on pause and me a newly ordained minister, I started to question some things. I couldn't fully understand why I was led to start the ministry if God wasn't going to support it. I started to question the entire last year, despite the evidence of what God was doing. *Was I really hearing from God? Were some things just coincidence? Did I do something wrong? Was giving so much money away the right thing to do? Where did I miss God in all of this?* I must honestly say it led me into a slump. Sometimes, I had to take a walk and ask God when things were going to start working right. My family members were looking up to me, and I was beginning to hope that God opened a way fast.

Wisdom and Understanding Note

Sometimes when following God, you will have periods where doubt will creep in. It happens to the best of us, but the key thing is not to act on that doubt. This also happened with Abraham and Sarah. Sarah suggested Abraham sleep with their maid because she didn't believe God would provide them with a child even after He promised He would. God still blessed them with the promised child in their old age. However, their doubt caused a problem that could have been prevented if they remained in faith and didn't act on their doubt.

To make my wife feel comfortable, I told her I would keep trying to make something happen. I also shared with her that we would live off the payments owed to us from the barbershop sale until God blessed the businesses. She had already been sacrificing so much, but she stood by me as I tried to be faithful and wholeheartily follow God.

February had passed, and it was close to the middle of March 2004. I was sitting at my parents' dining room table studying some marketing material on the computer. My father was in the kitchen preparing himself something to eat for dinner. Up until this time, he had never really said anything about the situation, but at times I could sense he wanted to say something. That night, as he walked past the dining room table to make his way upstairs with his plate of food, he stopped. He turned to me and asked what happened to my plans to be at the house for only a few weeks. By this time, it had been just about a year, and he wanted to know why my family and I were still living there. He began to share the increased expense of the bills in the house and wanted to know what I was doing.

This by far was the worst confrontation I had ever had as a man. I didn't even feel like a man. My parents didn't know that my wife and I had given away so much money. All they knew was that we were just staying there until we found a home to purchase. I was honestly keeping all that I was doing to myself, thinking God was going to open doors before it came down to this point. That night, I told my father the entire truth. I explained to him that I had given most of my money away, and I told him that I had invested in a few things, but none of it had gone anywhere. I told him I was waiting on God to bless me, so I could move out and that I no longer had any cash at all. After hearing all I said, my father looked at me as if I had three heads. He stared at me, and then just walked away from me, mumbling words under his breath.

I'm not sure why, but I felt so low. I was hurting inside and embarrassed. I know I was following God with all my heart, but something about this conversation with my father made me feel less than a man. Once my father reached the top of the steps, I went to the basement of the house and fell on my face on the floor, seeking God. I needed desperately to hear from God right away.

My parent's basement floor was an unfinished concrete basement floor. As I laid prostrate on the concrete, I began to ask God why the things He showed me were not happening. Why was I still at my parent's home? Why were the businesses not taking off? What was I doing wrong? I pleaded with God, over and over, to show me what I had to do. I had never prayed with so much passion and desperation before.

WHAT'S IN YOUR BACK POCKET?

After about ten minutes, I heard a voice tell me to be quiet and listen. I stayed on the floor, and God spoke directly to me. He asked me, "What's in your back pocket?" I had no idea what that meant. As I lay there in silence, He said it again, "What's in your back pocket?" I was still confused, but I began to reach around to feel my back pocket. As I did this a few times, I started to say, "My wallet is in my back pocket." God asked me again, and I responded, "My wallet is in my back pocket."

THE REVELATION WHILE IN PRAYER

Then the question became, "What do you keep in your wallet?" *Money!* I answered to myself. It was at that exact moment that God reminded me that I was supposed to give away *all* my money; I was not supposed to be keeping anything. Still on the floor, I was not 100% sure what it meant. I had given a large sum of the cash away and spent some on family and business. The last cash I had used for the ministry and ordination service. My cash was completely done. *What could God be talking about?* Then it hit me. I received the revelation of what God was saying.

I still had the balance of money owed to me from the sale of the barbershop. Even though this was a promissory note, it was still money I was to receive and represented the "all" that God told me to get rid of months ago. Once I understood in prayer what He pointed out, He then told me that, until I get rid of the money, my blessings wouldn't come. I don't think I even said, "Thank you, Jesus!" or "Amen" at that time. Once I heard what the Lord said and received my answer, I jumped up off the floor and ran upstairs to tell my wife the answer I had received in prayer.

I can remember running full speed up the stairs, calling my wife's name. "Melissa! Babe, where are you?" She came out of the room and, as we met at the top of the stairs, I said to her, "You know the money owed to us that we are holding onto while we are waiting on God to open doors?" She said, "Yes." I said, "Well, we have to give it away now because it is cursing us. Holding on to it is stopping our blessings." At that point, my wife had already seen me give all we had away. When I first started giving stuff and money away, there was little resistance on her part. However, when it came down to what I had just told her, she simply said, "Okay. Who do we give it to?" I told Melissa that God hadn't told me yet and that I would have to pray about it. That night, I fell asleep with complete clarity about what I needed to do.

CHAPTER 13

GOD SHOWED ME A SIGN

When I woke up the next morning and played back everything that had happened over the last year, up until the previous night, I started to feel a little guilty. Almost two months prior, I had told my wife we were going to live off the monthly payments in case God didn't do what He had said He would do for us. I beat myself up all day for allowing myself to think like that. God had already shown me, on numerous occasions, that He is faithful. But when it got down to the wire, I felt like I needed to hold on to at least a little something. What I learned was that meant I didn't have *TOTAL FAITH IN JESUS!*

Later in the afternoon, my mother came downstairs to where I was sitting at the dining room table. She told me that my father had told her what I had done. She had a few questions for me. The first thing she wanted to know was if it was all true. I replied, "Yes Mom, I gave the majority of my money away." She then said, "If God blessed you with all that money, why would you give it all away?" I said, "What if God gives it to you and then tells you to give it all away?" She looked at me, confused as to say, *Why would God tell you to do such a thing?* We made small talk afterward, but I could tell she did not fully understand why I had done what I did.

Around six that evening, a friend of mine called me. She was a prophetess in the ministry, and I hadn't spoken to her since my ordination service on February 7th. After saying, "Hello," she asked me about church. She asked, "When was the last time you went to church?" I told her I had not been to a service in weeks. I expressed how I had no desire to be in a church with how I had been feeling about my circumstances. To be honest, I was very discouraged and didn't want to be in a church at that time. She told me that I must go to church on Sunday because God had something for me. I really didn't know what "the something" was and she didn't say, but I felt strongly in my spirit that she was right. She instructed me to go to any church. She said it could be her church, my mother's church, or any random church, but I just needed to make sure I went to church on Sunday.

GOD SHOWED ME A SIGN - LITERALLY

When the prophetess shared that I could go to any church, I immediately saw the storefront sign for the church I needed to attend. After I hung up the phone, I told Melissa that I needed to attend church on Sunday. She asked me which church, and I told her I wasn't sure where but that I thought it was down Jamaica Avenue. Sunday morning came, and I was getting dressed and ready to go to church. At first, Melissa wasn't going to go with me. However, once I was dressed, she called downstairs and told me not to leave without her. So, we got the kids ready and we all headed towards Jamaica Avenue, which was two blocks away from my parents' home.

In Queens where we lived, Jamaica Avenue had two to three storefront churches on each block. I was planning to find the church on Jamaica Avenue with the same sign that I had seen in the vision. As we walked the first block, my wife asked me if each church we saw was the church in the vision, and I would answer, "No." This went on for two more blocks. As we reached the third block, we approached the first church on that block. She saw it and asked if this was the church I had seen in the vision. I paused for a second or two, staring at the sign and said, "Yes, this is the church." We opened the door and went inside.

We were late getting there, and the service had already started. We sat in the very last row, in what seemed to be the only seats available. A woman was preaching on something in reference to Moses. We stayed until the end of service, and when everyone was departing, she made her way over to my wife and me. She introduced herself as the pastor, and we spoke briefly. I didn't tell her anything about myself, nor did she ask, so she didn't know I was an ordained minister. We briefly spoke about the children and the church, and were about to part ways when she said she needed to tell us something. She said, "This week, God is going to bless you with one of the biggest blessings in your lives." She also said that we would be back to testify about it the following Sunday. My wife and I walked all the way home with excitement and anticipation of the word she had spoken over our lives.

On Monday morning, I was sitting at my computer, thinking about the word the pastor had spoken the day before. I was pondering all the possibilities that could come this week based on the word the woman of God had given us. Although nothing happened on that Monday, I was still excited because I had the rest of the week to see how God was going to come through. During the next few days, I waited in expectation for what God was going to do. This pastor had said *one of the biggest blessings*, so I was expecting nothing less.

Friday came, and the week was almost over. I started to get a little worried. My mind was starting to go places it shouldn't, and while I know God can do stuff at the last minute, surely, He wouldn't wait until Saturday night at 11:59 p.m. I didn't give up hope in the words she spoke just yet.

On Saturday morning, I thought to myself, *Today must be the day that God is going to reveal this big blessing to me.* I was figuring all day long that, since the big blessing hadn't happened yet, it would be coming that day. Every time the phone rang, I got excited. Whenever anyone left the house and came back, I was thinking they would come in with great news. I did this all day long while checking my computer every thirty minutes or so, to see if the blessing would come in an email.

Finally, *Saturday Night Live,* Live from New York, came on. I went to my wife and said, "We have 30 more minutes until this week is over and nothing has happened yet." We both were still waiting in expectation during the last 30 minutes of that week. I remember going back downstairs to my computer. I watched every minute on the computer screen while the time passed. I refreshed my email over and over, expecting an email to confirm the word spoken over us. Twelve O'clock struck and nothing. No phone call, no email, no knock at the door, or anything else to reveal the blessing the woman of God had spoken to us about. I waited until 1 a.m. to go back upstairs to share with Melissa that the woman of God had lied to us. I wrote the woman of God off as fake and concluded that the spirit of God hadn't spoken through her on Sunday when she spoke that word.

She had told me to come back to her church the following week because I would have a testimony. I had decided that I wouldn't be going back to her church because her prophecy had not come to pass. So, my wife and I stayed home and decided not to go there again. I take it very seriously when someone speaks a prophetic word. I always watch to see God confirm what He says through anyone or anything. She had spoken the word and put a time frame on it. I had waited for a week and nothing happened. At least that's what I thought!

Wisdom and Understanding Note

When you are hungry and want to be led by God, you are always looking for Him to speak to you. I take every word seriously because I have grown in the understanding that I need God to be everything I'm supposed to be. When God spoke to me about my error in holding the last money, I was listening right away to see where He wanted me to give it. When the Prophetess Shepherd called me and told me I needed to go to church, I was there the following Sunday. God showed me a storefront church sign, and I sought it out. God is not limited in his communication to man; we just have to be willing and obedient for him to reward us greatly. **"If you are willing and obedient, you shall eat the good of the land;" Isaiah 1:19 NKJV**

Tuesday came, and I was once again at the dining room table, working on the computer. I'm not sure what I was working on, but I heard the voice of the Lord speak very clearly to me. He said, "You know the woman pastor you just met? I want you to give her the rest of the money that you have." I knew for sure that I heard God speak to me. I immediately ran upstairs to tell my wife what God had just said. I went into the room and said, "Babe, God just told me where to give the last of our money." She replied, "To the woman pastor we just met last week?" That blew my mind! She knew before I had even told her. God had told my wife as well. This was confirmation for both of us. I was 100% sure that the pastor we had just met was to receive the money. I couldn't wait to sow the money into her ministry.

TWO ROTTWEILERS ATTACKING ME

Thursday of that same week, I had the strangest dream. It was around 6 a.m., and I was sleeping next to my wife. I didn't realize I was dreaming, but I was wrestling with two Rottweilers. They started to get the best of me, and I woke up just as they started to bite me. The dream was so real that I sat up in bed and asked my wife if she had seen what happened. She told me I must have been dreaming. My bed was next to the window, and I lifted the blinds to see if I could see any dogs in my neighbor's yard. I was sweating and couldn't believe how real the dream had been. I laid back down and wondered why the dream seemed so real. I would soon find out what the dream was all about.

SUNDAY MORNING BACK TO CHURCH

On Sunday morning, I couldn't wait to get the last bit of money out of my hands. My wife and I got ready to go to church and started to make our way up the street. As we were walking up the street, my wife seemed like she was trying to tell me something. She said, "Babe, since we have been living at your parents' house all this time, maybe we should instead give the money we have left to your parents." This started an argument right on the spot. I asked her why she would try to go against what God spoke when she had also received confirmation about what God told both of us. I told her that God hadn't told me to give the money to my parents. He had told me to sow the seed into the woman of God's church. So, we walked a bit further, until my wife was back in agreement with me.

We finally arrived at the church and made our way to some available seats. As soon as I sat down, the pastor called me up to the front. She said, "Young man, I told you when you come back, you would have a testimony for me; so please come and share your testimony." I walked to the front of the church, and honestly, I didn't know what she wanted me to share since nothing had happened. (The truth was that it had already happened, and I didn't know it). I first introduced myself as an Elder and let the church know I was a minister. I then told her and the congregation what I had done in the previous twelve months, and how I had followed God's instructions by giving all my money away. When I had finished speaking, I told her that God sent me back to her church to sow a seed. I explained to her, in front of everyone, how I had just over $17,000 owed to me from the sale of my barbershop. I told her the Lord had told me to give it to her and that she was to use the money however she saw fit to use it. She simply said, "Okay." It was at that moment that I realized I had forgotten the paperwork at home. After the service, I told her that I would have to go home and get the documents and that I would be right back.

We went home to grab the paperwork. My wife decided to stay home with the kids, and I walked back over to the church. Once

I arrived back at the church, the pastor was sitting there waiting for me, alongside a deacon and an elder of the church. I explained to her again that I had sold my shop and had a balance of the sale owed to me. The documents already had a page where I could sign the note over to someone else, and that was exactly what we did. I signed it over to her and she would now be receiving the remainder of the money owed to me.

Once the assignment was completed, she asked what I did for a living. I explained that I was trying to get businesses off the ground and that I currently had an audio series where I talked over hip hop beats. When I said that, her eyebrows went up and she replied that her son was a music producer and that he also made hip hop beats. I asked her who her son was, and she said, "My son is Rockwilder."

GOD, WHAT ARE YOU DOING?

As I looked at the pastor, I could see the resemblance. I knew Rockwilder as one of the biggest producers in Hip Hop. As a hip-hop producer, I had often studied his music, which could be found on the biggest hip-hop albums. I didn't know what God was doing, but I know He was doing something. I felt it right away, as soon as she said it. I started feeling in my spirit that God was going to make good on His promise. I just didn't know-how.

We exchanged contact information, and I started walking back home. As I walked, I just kept saying, "God, what are you doing?" Deep down in my spirit, I knew God was honoring His promise to me, but I didn't know exactly how. I finally reached home, and I couldn't wait to tell my wife.

As I came into the house, I called out, "Melissa, where you at?" She was in the kitchen, and I didn't waste any time telling her. I said, "Babe, you know the woman we just sowed that seed with?" She said, "Yes." I said, "That is Rockwilder's mother!" She replied, "Who is Rockwilder?"

I had to break it down to her. She had no clue. I started naming songs she may have heard on the radio, songs by Beyoncé, Jay-z, Missy Elliot, Pink, Mya, and the many others he had made hits for. She knew many of the songs but didn't know his name as the one who produced the music. I told her, "God is doing something, I just don't know what."

Wisdom and Understanding Note

I was excited to give the money away because I knew for sure that I had heard from the Lord in prayer. He told me long ago that when I did my part, He would do his part. Many of us fail because we don't totally believe God will do His part. Please let me encourage you if that is you. **"The earth *is* the LORD's, and all its fullness, the world and those who dwell therein. For He has founded it upon the seas, And established it upon the waters." Psalm 24:1 NKJV.** When you listen to God, He can make anything happen for you. The earth and everything in it is His.

CHAPTER 14

EATING OUT OF GOD'S HAND!

I was completely broke and didn't have any more money. I had given my last dollar away. Even though it had taken some time since God had first told me to give it all away, I had finally gotten to that point where I was emptied out. I was totally waiting for God to make everything happen for me.

The following Wednesday, Bishop Stinson called and invited me over to her home to have a sit-down. I gladly accepted the invite and was looking forward to meeting her there. She told me to bring copies of the audio series I had recorded; so before I left, I grabbed a few copies and went on my way.

This meeting allowed us to get more acquainted. As I sat in her dining room, I was immediately drawn to the plaques hanging on her walls. On display were several Gold and Platinum records that her son, Rockwilder, had produced. It was pretty impressive. She asked me how long I had been a minister and what I was currently doing in ministry. So, I shared with her that I had started having meetings during the past December and explained how I didn't have the money to continue to finance the location we were using. She told me that I was welcome to worship at her church and be an associate minister there. I told her I would visit a few times and let her know. The following Sunday, my family and I visited the church. We enjoyed the service from beginning to end and decided we would attend until God said differently.

MEETING ROCKWILDER

During all this time, I had not yet met Rockwilder. The following Tuesday, April 13, Bishop Stinson called to tell me that her older son had died. She asked me to come over to the family home that night, and I did.

Once I walked in and greeted everyone in the living room, I made my way over to the dining room. There were a lot of people in the house, including a few other people that I knew already from the neighborhood. Bishop Stinson was sitting at the dining room table grieving the loss of her son. I reached out to give her a hug of comfort, and she followed by telling someone to give me their seat at the table. As I sat down, she looked to the other side of the table and said, "Elder Brown, this is my Son, Rockwilder." I hadn't noticed him but as I turned towards him, he reached his hand out to greet me and said, "Nice to meet you." It was a sad occasion to meet Rockwilder. Even though he was talking to everyone, at times he would space out for a few minutes. I'm assuming he was thinking about his brother who had just passed. It was just a sad situation.

THE BIRTH OF ROCBEATS.COM

Three days later, on Friday, I was in my parent's house telling my wife that there had to be a big reason why God had connected me to Rockwilder. I told her that night that I thought Rockwilder and I were going to start a business online. I shared with her that we would sell his beats to make money on the Internet, and

I would set it all up. The first thing she said was, "How do you know he will even do such a thing?" Sometimes my wife likes to play devil's advocate. It can be annoying, but I have learned that it's needed to balance me. It allows me to think more deeply about my plans. I just gave her a crazy look, as I sometimes do. At that moment, it popped into my head: Rockbeats.com

I went right over to my computer to do a domain name search to see if the name was available. The original spelling as Rockbeats.com was not available. However, Rocbeats.com without the "K" was. So that is the name I attempted to register. I say attempted because, once I got to the checkout, it kept declining my card.

I dialed up customer support to let them know I was having an issue with the checkout. The guy on the other end of the phone told me that it was no problem and that he would help me register the domain name. I wasn't 100% sure why the card wasn't working when all I needed was $14.99, and I was using a debit card that had $19 left on it.

When I told him the name I was trying to register, he replied to me and said, "This wouldn't happen to be for the music producer Rockwilder." I started laughing and said, "Yes, it is." He began to share how he knew of his music and that he was a fan. Knowing that I hadn't said anything to Rockwilder about the idea yet, I believe this was God giving me the confirmation that it was a green light.

> **Wisdom and Understanding Note**
>
> God has a way of letting you know that you are on the right path. Once He speaks something to you, look for it to be confirmed. What you will notice is that, once you open your heart to receive confirmation, He will speak to you through almost anything or anyone. I had a tech issue for a reason and had no choice but to speak with a tech support agent. Once I shared the problem I was having and the domain name, he brought up Rockwilder. Out of all the companies and operators I could have reached that day, I was put in contact with one that questioned me about the abbreviated name "Roc."

ROCKWILDER MAKING SPAGHETTI

The following Friday, Bishop Stinson had invited my family over for dinner. Rockwilder was in the kitchen making spaghetti for everyone when we arrived. Once he was done, he came out to talk to everyone. (The spaghetti was actually good by the way.) He soon made his way over to me, and we began to chop it up. As we began to share a few things about ourselves with each other, I asked him if he thought we could do business together. Without hesitation, he said, "Yes." I told him that I was a web developer, and we could launch a website on the Internet. He agreed, and I told him about the website idea for Rocbeats.com.

EVERYTHING IS NOT ALWAYS EASY

I now had the green light and an opportunity to work with a certified legend in the Hip Hop business, so things should be looking up for me and my family now. Not so fast! I believe God had some more things for me to learn before He allowed me to move forward.

I had no money, and I had no intention of asking Rockwilder for any money. I would do my part to start working on the website, and then get him to start supplying the music so that we could launch. Things always work out in your head first much better than when it's time to execute your plan.

In the previous year, around mid-2003, I discovered that Indie producers were selling their music on the internet. As a music producer, I had noted the few who were doing it. What many of them had done was sell non-exclusive beats for high prices, -- in the range of $100 - $250. When I first saw it, I thought that it was kind of pricey. It had given me the idea to give it a go since my friend, Greg, had given me the music production software, and I was making the beats I had made for the Legal Hustling Series. I later changed my mind and didn't pursue it. At that time, I didn't see how I could scale it up to make the money I wanted to be making. Fast forward almost a year later and having a partner like Rockwilder, I saw that the possibilities would be different because of who he was. The only bad part about it was that Rockwilder didn't see it that way.

Rockwilder was a brand in hip hop, getting anywhere from $10,000 to $25,000 upfront for his music, which was from record labels buying exclusive rights. Here I come with an idea that he could start selling non-exclusive beats on the internet for $25 - $50 each (Non-exclusive means the same beat can sell repeatedly, a million times). I had a lot of resistance from Rockwilder because he couldn't see himself doing that with his name. At the time, his managers couldn't see it either, and that kind of put my idea on ice. I couldn't see how they couldn't see how selling the same beat over and over, even 10,000 times on the Internet, while still keeping the ownership rights to the music, wasn't a good idea.

> ## Wisdom and Understanding Note
>
> Your vision will not always be easy to sell to others. It shouldn't discourage you because it is your vision and God showed it to you. However, as you keep moving in your vision, you will need to exercise patience until those around you either catch up or fall away.

GOD'S PROCESS FOR SUCCESS

With the going back and forth with Rock and being around him, we started to learn more and more about each other. It was actually a good thing. I didn't stop working on the website, but I did a little development work on it here and there.

In mid-May of 2004, Bishop Stinson asked me to preach for the first time at the church. I can't remember what I preached, but I do remember that the church blessed me with a love offering of $100. It was very much needed as I had to purchase some food for my family. As an associate minister at the church, I would preach every 3rd or 4th week as needed.

GOD SHOWS HIS FAITHFULNESS WITH ICE CREAM

My son Isaiah's birthday party was coming up, and there was no ice cream for the party we were having for him. I had spent money on the cake and a few other things but somehow forgot to buy ice cream. My wife informed me that there was no ice cream and that we needed some for the kids who were there. I didn't have any money for ice cream, but I heard the Holy Spirit telling me to just get into my mother's car and drive to the ice cream shop. I decided, in my heart, that I was going to listen to the Holy Spirit. On my way to the store, I started thinking of ways that I could convince the person at the counter to give me the ice cream for free. I thought that I would put on a sad face and beg the person. I would tell him or her I had many kids at my house begging for ice cream. I dreamed up a few scenarios before I entered the store.

When I arrived at the ice cream store, there was a lady in the store and a man behind the counter. For some reason, I decided to wait for the lady to leave before I approached the man behind the counter. Just to stall, I went to the freezer where pre-made ice cream cakes were and acted like I was shopping for a cake. I planned to walk to the counter and basically tell the guy my story after the other customer left. I didn't care if I needed to sob and cry for him to hear my plea. I was prepared to do anything for him to give me the ice cream.

When the lady left the store, I walked over to the counter where the man was standing. In front of him was a freezer where they kept the pre-packed ice cream I needed for the party. I thought at first, that I would tell the guy my story, and then see if he would let me grab the ice cream from the freezer for free. As I walked toward the counter, something (Holy Spirit) told me to reach in the freezer and put the ice-cream on the counter first. I followed the voice and did just that.

I opened the freezer to pick two quarts of ice cream. On top of one of the ice creams was a $10 bill. I was extremely surprised! I wondered who could have left a $10 bill inside of the freezer, but I knew only God could have known I was coming to the ice cream shop without cash and that I would be opening that particular freezer. I picked the ice cream up and gave the guy the $10 to pay for it. I remember looking around the empty store still in shock, thinking who must have put that there. This was God showing me that I could trust Him, no matter what. I could trust Him to eat directly out of His hand.

Wisdom and Understanding Note

Many times, before this moment, I would feel a "some kind of way" when I lost money. Particularly cash that would fall out of my pocket. My ice cream story gave me a different perspective. The money you lose may just provide some happiness at a children's party! LOL

One of the things my wife and I had decided not to do was ask my parents for any money. We were grateful for the shelter they provided, but we didn't want to burden them with the decisions we made. We started discovering ways to stretch meals to make them last longer. Stocking up on rice and cutting chicken breasts into small pieces, and then adding gravy to make it last for a few days at a time. God was teaching us, and we were learning how to make things work with very little resources.

Summer had come and was just about over. It had been about six months since Rockwilder and I was divinely connected. Rockwilder was still not 100 percent on board with the concept I had, and I was sitting at my parents' house, still believing God. I was fully committed to waiting on God to make it happen when the time was right. However, the truth was it's not easy to wait on God and only eat out of His hand when He provides. I can remember having to take long walks to ease my mind of the stress that would build up. However, as I was going through the process, I was getting better and better with the patience I needed to have full trust in God.

Wisdom and Understanding Note

Anything that you're going to receive from God will require patience. You must know that if you are going to follow God, that He sets things up in his timing. I was dying daily to myself and learning how to be okay when I didn't see God moving. Once you learn this trait and realize that God is in complete control, it will reduce stress and make you feel less anxious about any situation you can't control. Remember, God is pulling all the strings for you in His timing. Just Be Still! **"Be still, and know that I am God;" Psalm 46:10**

IS THIS $100,000 A YEAR FROM GOD?

I received a call from a long-time barbershop client whom I had not spoken to since I sold the shop. He was a good client who also left great tips. He had called to see what I had been doing since I left the shop. He knew that I was putting down the clippers and wanted to know what I was doing with myself. After I told him, he then let me know the real reason for his call.

This client was the son of a rich mortgage banker who had a mortgage bank in Long Island. He knew that before I sold my shop, that I had been studying the mortgage business and left for a while to try it out. Around that time, he had also told his father about me and said that I could possibly work with his father. At the time, I declined and really didn't pursue the opportunity to work with anyone else. So, it never went any further than that. However, what he shared with me on this call was that his father wanted to meet with me. He had an opportunity in their business for key personnel with the processing of mortgages.

From another one of my friends who knew the family personally, I received the inside scoop. I learned that his father, who owned a mortgage bank, was making four to five million dollars every year in that business.

He told me on the phone to come to the office on Long Island and speak with his father. He told me that he had shared with his dad that I was a businessman with a few barbershops and had worked in the field already. He said that his dad was willing to pay $100,000 a year for a person like me who could help in the business. Once he shared everything with me, I told him I would meet with his dad, and we set up a time and date for the following week.

As I sat home and really started to think about this offer, I started to realize that even though I was broke, it wouldn't be the right thing for me to do. I know what I had prayed for. If I pursued this opportunity, one, I would be putting myself back into a position that I had prayed to get myself out of and two, I would have no time to build my own company that would offer me the freedom to do what I wanted with my own time.

Wisdom and Understanding Note

Watch out for the pitfalls that completely block you from reaching your vision. I see it all the time. People take jobs or

> pursue income opportunities because of how much more money they can make. If you are not chasing anything or trying to reach a desired target in life, then your actions will not matter. However, if you are trying to build a life where your time and freedom are important, then you cannot jump on every opportunity that doesn't align with the vision. Many of those distractions will zap you of all the energy and time you need to work on your own vision. So that $100,000, even though I was broke, was not for me-- which also means I passed the test!

Since I made the appointment, and it was an opportunity, I asked my mother if she wanted to meet with my friend's father. My mother had a background in real estate and was a licensed agent years ago. I thought maybe she would be good in the mortgage business. I told her that all she needed to do was learn about mortgage financing and that she could possibly get the job. She agreed, so I called my friend and asked if my mother could interview instead. He confirmed that she could meet with his father.

I drove with my mother to the interview, and while she went into the office, I remained outside in the parking lot. When she came back, she told me that he liked her but that he really wanted to work with me. She asked me why I wouldn't take the offer. I explained that I couldn't take it because I was waiting on God to give me exactly what I wanted. My vision was to generate lots of income on the Internet and build my own. If I allowed the mortgage job to distract me, I wouldn't get to see the blessing I had prayed for. I don't know if my mother understood what I was saying, but I was very convinced that I should wait for God.

> **Wisdom and Understanding Note**
>
> I believe that, once you know better, you do better, and I was fully committed to building my own life. Gaining full control of your life takes focusing on building your own empire. My mindset is that I'd rather be the one who is hiring. Being in that position means building your own life brick by brick.

CHRISTMAS IS COMING

The struggle was still very real, and it was getting close to the Thanksgiving holiday. My wife and I were still finding ways to be creative in stretching each dollar we received. It was a blessing that the kids were young and didn't really require that much. We had all boys, so the younger two got the hand-me-downs from the older ones.

We had no money and were thinking about what we would do for the Christmas holiday. Around the first week of December, a $1200 check came for me in the mail. I was completely shocked because I didn't have anyone or business that I knew of that owed me any money. As I read the letter that came with the check, I discovered that, when I sold my home, there was a miscalculation at the closing and $1200 was owed to me. The letter explained that it had taken so long to get to me because there was no address left for anyone to locate me. As to how they had learned that I was at my mother's house, I'm not 100% sure. But I credit it all to God for holding it for a time until it was needed. The family and I had a blessed holiday season because of the financial oversight. I knew that their oversight was God's INSIGHT!

MONEY IN THE STREETS!

By February, we had used the entire twelve hundred dollars. It had been almost a year since I had met Rockwilder, and he still had not come around 100% with the concept I had for the website. During this time, however, I was still studying and developing my web programming skills.

One day, I was sitting on my computer when my wife told me we had to come up with $85 for something one of the kids needed. I can't remember what it was, but I do remember being a little frustrated. After she left, I prayed to God about my concerns. After I prayed, I told my wife that I needed to take a drive. I had absolutely nowhere to go but just felt the need to drive and clear my head. I grabbed the keys to my mother's car and left.

Driving is something I often do to clear my mind. As I drove around Queens, I came to an intersection. At the corner, I was stopped by the red light. A lady suddenly pulled on the back door of the car and asked if I was the cab driver. I told her that I wasn't. However, she kept insisting that she was supposed to be meeting a cab at the corner and that I was the cab driver. I asked her where she was headed, and she said that she was on her way to Brooklyn. I asked her how much she paid to go from Queens to Brooklyn, and she said $25. I immediately told her to get into the car and said, "I AM YOUR CAB!"

I drove her to Brooklyn, and she gave me a $10 tip. I began going to this corner to pick up passengers for what is called *gypsy cabbing*. I knew what I was doing wasn't legal, but I started providing for my family and earning money to get the things we needed.

I no longer wanted to take chances with my mother's car, so I started looking for something affordable to continue the cab hustle. I remembered that my cousin, Michele, had a 2002 Nissan Altima she had parked. I asked her about it, and she said I could have it for $600. I gave her $200, and she let me pay off the rest later. That car became my new way to get money. It allowed me to keep my freedom and be totally flexible to keep my focus while waiting for the real promise of God.

Wisdom and Understanding Note

A side hustle beats a job any day when you have a vision. If you are trying to focus on building real dreams in your life, a regular job may hinder you. Your commitment is to the vision you have, not the job that will burn you out and not offer the time you need to build it and succeed.

CHAPTER 15

THE PROMISE

It's late September 2005, and my wife tells me we are expecting a new addition. This would be baby number four. I always knew that we wanted to try again because we already had three boys, and one more roll of the dice could bring a baby girl, but this was not the perfect time. At least that was what we were thinking. I would have preferred to be living in our own home. My thoughts every day after was that something has got to break so I could get my family in their own home.

November 2005 came around, and it had now been a year and eight months since God had connected me with Rockwilder. Plenty of times, I felt like I was going to throw in the towel and give up on pursuing the partnership. However, deep down in my spirit, I always replayed how we were connected. There had to be a reason why God had me blindly sow my last money into his mother's church not even knowing he was connected there.

Around the beginning of November, Rockwilder called me to see what I was doing. He was at his home in Long Island and said that if I wasn't doing anything, I should come to visit. Later that night, we linked up.

Often throughout the last year of our relationship, Rockwilder would hit me up and share things that he was going through. It was at these times that I felt more like a spiritual adviser to him. The things that we discussed can never be repeated, but I will say that many people took advantage of him financially and were only in his life to take away from, and not to add to.

As we talked that day, he began to share some of his frustration with the music business. Out of nowhere, he said to me, "Let's do the website now." I was not expecting him to say that!

GIVE ME YOUR BEATS!

I immediately told him, "Give me your beats!" He connected a hard drive to his computer, grabbed a stack of CD's from his kitchen and started playing beat after beat. As he was playing each beat, he told me who he made each beat for. Somehow or another, they didn't either get the beat or had heard the beat and decided not to use it. Rockwilder had done beats for Nas, Jay-Z, LL Cool J, Redman, Eminem, and the list goes on. I couldn't believe the sound of the beats they had turned down. Each beat was pure GOLD!

He ended up giving me about 65 beats to start rocbeats.com. Even though I wanted more, it was more than enough to get the website up and running. I can remember driving back from Long Island playing the beats in the car and saying to myself, *It's about to be on.*

Many months had passed since I first had the idea for rocbeats.com. The website was 90% developed and just sitting on my computer, waiting for the green light. I only had a few things to do before I could launch the website.

ROCBEATS WEBSITE LAUNCH CHECKLIST

My goal was to get the website launched in the first week of December. With about three weeks to go, I started to finalize the home page design of the website. I uploaded clips of all the beats so visitors could hear snippets. I ran numerous tests to make sure the beats could be purchased without issue. Lastly, I started putting together the marketing scheme to ensure that I could reach the Hip Hop and R&B demographic I needed to respond to and buy the beats.

Everything was ready to launch with only a week to go. I was a bit nervous but not scared to move forward. I had still been doing cab rides to make ends meet. On the last day of November 2005, I was driving down to the spot where I would normally grab a cab fare. As I was about to approach, something in me spoke out loud, "$10 Beats." I immediately turned my car around and raced back home to make some last-minute changes.

I had been all set to launch the website and was setting the prices for the beat leases to be $50 - $100. As I was driving, something kept bugging me. I wasn't sure what, but I felt something wasn't right. Then I thought to myself, if I was going to sell thousands of the same beats over and over, $50 wouldn't work. Above $50 would give buyer resistance and not create a buying frenzy. I needed a fast word of mouth phenomenon to move the beats like hotcakes. Then it hit my spirit, "$10." I changed the press release and the website to promote all the beats for $10. Now I had a promotion I felt would be too good to be true. That night, I started sending the press release everywhere, hoping it would be covered in as many publications as possible.

ROCBEATS.COM LAUNCHES

On December 1, 2005, rocbeats.com was officially launched. The website did very well in sales in the first month. I ran the $10 sale for each beat, and within a couple of months, thousands of beats sold and continued to sell.

Rockwilder started getting feedback from all over the music industry. Major record industry executives were coming up to him and giving him props for launching something they had never seen before. Fans were coming up to him in the streets and thanking him for releasing a website where they could work with someone of his caliber.

I started getting interview requests from all over the country, from radio stations and magazines. They wanted to report on Rockwilder and his new website, Rocbeats.com. The site was growing bigger and bigger. As I tracked the progress and growth of the site, I often checked the traffic to see where website visitors were coming from. This put me on to many indie music producer websites that had chat forums. As I observed the threads and read the comments, I saw that many of the music producers were voicing their disgust with rocbeats.com. They were complaining that major producers were going to start coming online and taking their beat sales. I honestly didn't think anything of that because if you were a good music producer and knew how to market, you could do very well on the internet. However, I read a thread in which many of the producers were saying Rockwilder was a horrible producer. Now, of course, I didn't think that at all, especially when Rockwilder was responsible for more than 70 million record sales at that time, but, I wanted to share it with Rockwilder so that he could get a kick out of it.

I didn't waste any time reaching out to him. I called Rockwilder around 1 a.m. and let him know what I was reading. "I will battle all of them," is what he told me. My response was, "You will" and told him I would get back to him. The next day, I called him and told him I had registered RocBattle.com so that he could now battle them. I broke it down for him how the website could be set up to grow. I also shared that we would need to hire programmers because what we needed was a little more than I knew how to do at that time.

As we moved forward, I was learning things along the way. In March 2006, Rockwilder was invited to visit BET (Black Entertainment Television). He was going to judge one of the freestyle Fridays. That was an event in which two rappers would battle each other in front of the studio audience and three celebrity judges. I made sure that he had a Rocbeats.com shirt on. When the show aired, the website crashed. There had been so much traffic to the website that it overloaded. I had a small hosting company that couldn't handle all the web traffic, so as the traffic started coming in, the server was overloaded and shut down every website the company had on their system. I learned a very expensive lesson because the website was shut down for four days. I now make sure that I host all my web business on dedicated servers that can handle high traffic at any time.

Rocbeats 2006 Promo Photo

Rocbeats 2006 Promo Pictures
Rockwilder and Al aka Fat Fingers

Rocbeats.com 2006 Screenshot

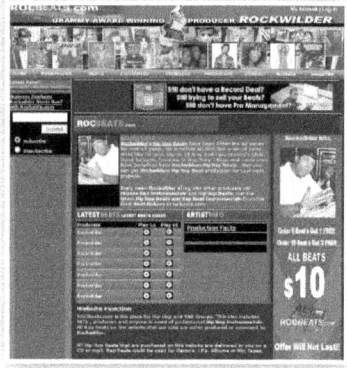

ROCBATTLE WEBSITE LAUNCH CHECKLIST

After the launch of Rocbeats.com, there was a team of programmers from Canada who reached out to me. They wanted to know if they could use some of the Rockwilder beats for a website they had developed. I respectfully declined but told them that I would be in touch with them if anything changed. Things changed when Rockwilder agreed to do the beat battle website, so I gave them a call.

I shared the beat battle website idea with them. Once they heard what we wanted to do, they wanted to be a part of it right away. They told me they would get back to me with a quote in a few days. They quoted us $30,000, which would cover the complete development of the website. At that moment, it was way more than I wanted to spend. Besides, I wasn't 100% sure the site would take off. I offered them a monthly commission from the income the site would generate, in exchange for maintaining all technical aspects of the website. Also, it would mean they would complete all new web development and upgrades that the website would need. They agreed and we set a launch date for May 1, 2006. I spent eight dollars on a GoDaddy domain registration to get started on the Rocbattle.com venture

$8 INVESTMENT TURNS INTO MILLIONS

Ten days before we launched Rocbattle.com, my wife came to tell me that baby number four was knocking at the door. The fourth addition is now here and it's another baby boy, *Micaiah!* Unlike the feeling I had before, I was a lot more confident with all the recent business developments.

I could remember getting everything all set for the rocbattle launch. It had taken the programmers about three months to finish all the programming and design details. I gave it a test run and all was ready to go. I had completed the press release around that time and was ready to send it to all the hip hop blogs. It was the only method I was going to use to announce the launch. It was the same method I had used to get rocbeats.com started. I released the news to over twenty of the major websites the night before the launch. What happened next was pretty amazing.

With everything in motion, we opened the doors, and over 600 members signed up for Rocbattle on the first day. Music producers from all over the world were uploading their beats and battling each other from day one. With the features we offered, they were positioned to sell their beats on the website to visitors all around the world. The site started to grow extremely--so fast that celebrities in the industry were finding new talent on Rocbattle to work with. Many young and talented music producers became well known within the music business. A few of them went on afterward to reach millions of sales with major artists in the music business.

The beat battles tournaments on the site would offer grand cash prizes of $2000 to the music producer who made it to the last round of 64 music producers going head to head. These battles created some intense moments on the website.

THE PERKS OF HANGING OUT WITH ROCKWILDER

Having a partner and friend like Rockwilder had many benefits. It was cool to be out and about and see someone recognize Rockwilder and ask him, "Are you Rockwilder?" I remember going through the drive-through at McDonald's when the cashier window opened up and the guy said, "Hey, aren't you Rockwilder?" Rockwilder would always have a humble reply and say, "Yes, What's Up!" That day at McDonald's was funny to me because before you knew it, like 4-5 workers were sticking their head out the server window. Rockwilder would always be humble about it.

The majority of the nights we hung out, there were almost always other celebrities we would bump into. The biggest celebs in the business would see Rockwilder and call him out. He stands at 6 ft 4, so he's not hard to miss. There were a lot of celebrities I met and got to hang out with for a night as a result of being connected to him. Although I can go on and share many stories, I will tell you about two nights that I often remember.

THE NIGHT IN FRONT OF SONY MUSIC STUDIOS

One night after a studio session at Sony Studios in Manhattan, Rockwilder and myself were standing outside in front of the building. I can't recall why we were standing in place, but there was another person who had just left from speaking to us. About five minutes went by and then an all-black suburban truck slowly started to creep up to us. The truck windows were all tinted, so we couldn't see inside. It was a warm summer night and it was late, so my thoughts were the negative first. It was kind of awkward because the truck sat in the middle of the street for about a minute or more. I knew I was in Manhattan, which was in a safer part of New York, but if you're from certain parts and you know the streets, your hood antennas start to signal, *this may not be good!*

I looked at Rockwilder a few times, then looked at the truck. It seems like he was doing the same thing to me. It was at the point when I was about to tell him lets go that the back window came down. It was like a movie because when the window came down, you still didn't see who it was. So, while we are still standing there as if we were on pause in a video game, a head pops out the window and screams, "What's up Rock." I immediately knew who it was;

Alicia Keys. She is laughing because she saw our reaction. I gave off a little giggle because I didn't think it was that funny.

Rockwilder walks off the curb and greets her with a hug. They start talking about music and her next album she was working on. She told him she was taking submissions for the project and they were going to be finished with the album soon. So, they discussed getting in contact for a meeting later. She then turns toward me to joke about what just happened and notice that Rockwilder and I had on the same shirts. So, Rockwilder signals for me to come in the street and says, "This is my partner, Allen Brown."

Alicia asks me why we had on the same shirts. So, I started to tell her they were shirts promoting the new website we had 'Rocbattle.com.' After a little more small talk and me cracking jokes, I started joking with her, asking her to battle on the site. She continues laughing, never taking me seriously the whole time, but I continue joking around, making her laugh.

When she pulled off, Rockwilder was like, "Can't believe you were making her laugh like that." I told him I was trying to get her to do at least one battle on rocbattle. A million people would have known about the website overnight. We just laughed about it and went on our way. The majority of times, there was always a highlight of the night.

ANOTHER NIGHT TO REMEMBER

Rockwilder rings my phone and lets me know that his friend, Janet Jackson, was in town promoting her new album. Rockwilder had caught the attention of Janet with his hit song, "Da Rockwilder." Janet specifically sought him out and flew him to her home in

California. He was blessed to do five songs on her 2001 "All For You" album.

Janet was in Manhattan promoting her 20 Y.O. anniversary album. This was around September of 2006. We arrived at the club to a line of people that stretched all the way down the block. It seemed like there were people all over the place. I'm following Rockwilder as he is walking straight up to the door where the bouncers are. It's like three huge guys standing at the door. Rockwilder signals a guy that was standing on the side to get the attention of someone else. Once that person turned around and saw it was Rockwilder, he signaled the bouncers to let us in.

Once inside the club, there was hardly anywhere to move to. The front is jammed packed to where no one could even move. Rockwilder turned and told me we were headed to the VIP and to stay close to him. As we began to push our way through the crowd, I started to see people recognize who he was. The funny thing is the few women that kept grabbing at him. He just kept pushing through, looking back every so often to see where I was at.

As we were getting closer to the back, we finally reached what I believe was the first VIP section. Two big guys dressed in all black were blocking the entrance. Once they noticed Rockwilder, they moved to the side to let him in, but quickly went to move back in position to block me. It was at that moment that Rockwilder turned around and said, "He is with me," and they let me in.

Once inside this VIP area, we are immediately greeted by a guy named Chaka who, at that time, managed the rapper, Ludacris. We had already bumped into him and Ludacris earlier that night at dinner. They both were in the VIP section, along with other notable celebrities. I grabbed a seat while Rockwilder went over to talk to

Swizz Beatz. After about ten minutes, Rockwilder came over to me and said, "Let's go in the other VIP section with Janet."

As we walked over toward her way, we came up to another two big guys dressed in all black. When she looked up and saw us, she said "Hey Rock!" The two guys moved to the side. Rockwilder had greeted Janet with a hug and they began to talk like they were buddies. After a minute, he introduced me to her. "Janet, I want you to meet my partner, Allen Brown." She reached her hand out and said, "Nice to meet you, Allen Brown." All jokes aside, it seemed like this part was in slow motion. I was shaking her hand saying, "This is Penny from Good Times."

I have been around plenty of celebs before I met Rockwilder, as well as those I met while with Rockwilder, but Janet Jackson was a little different. That pretty much was the highlight of that night. They continued to converse a little bit more before we left that section, but the entire time after the handshake, I was staring at her. It was like all her hit songs and videos were playing in my head, LOL. Another great night to remember.

Rocbattle 2006 Promo Photo

Rocbattle.com 2007 Screenshot

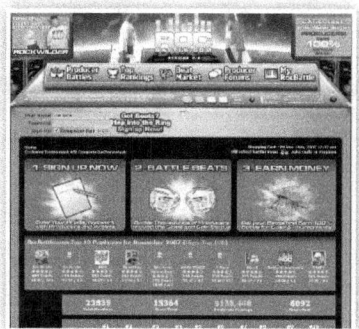

THANK YOU, LORD, FOR ROCBATTLE.COM

The website ran from 2006 to 2014 and paid out millions of dollars to producers worldwide. It had become one of the main locations for artists to buy beats on the internet. The website grew to over 130 thousand members and at times paid out over $40,000 a month in commissions to music producers. The site is still up today, but the beat battle scene has slowed down over the years. I will be looking to revamp the site and offer cash prizes upwards of $10,000 in the very near future.

After 2014, I started to focus on other projects. In addition, around that time, many other competitors had started to enter the online beat selling space. From May 2006 up until 2014, the site generated a very nice income for me. I'm extremely grateful that millions of dollars were made, and I ultimately had all the freedom in the world to be with my family anytime I wanted while generating income online.

Shortly after everything took off, my wife and I started getting confirmation from the Lord about moving to Pennsylvania. So we waited for the school year to end and then made our way to Pennsylvania where we have been living for over 13 years. While living in Pennsylvania, we purchased our own home in 2012. I still continued to generate income on the internet with several online businesses.

CHAPTER 16

EXCEEDINGLY MORE

We serve a God who can do more than we ask or think. **"Now unto him that is able to do exceedingly abundantly above all that we ask or think, according to the power that worketh in us." Ephesians 3:20.** When I asked Rockwilder if he wanted to do business with me, I didn't think in a million years that so many income opportunities would come out of it. When I asked God to help me turn my businesses around and give me time to be with my family, I had no idea He would take me on the ride that He did. It has been truly an amazing journey. He continued to bless me with even more income opportunities--all because of the seeds I sowed and believing God for the change.

ROCKWILDER RINGTONES

I can't remember the exact name of the company but when we released our first website, RocBeats.com, a ringtone company reached out to me. They wanted to know if the beats we posted on Rocbeats.com could be used for their ringtone company. After I did a little research on them, I set up a meeting.

The company was in Manhattan near the Wall Street area. This was the first meeting I attended on behalf of the business I had with Rockwilder. The company wanted to pay Rockwilder upfront for some beats they could use and then, also give him residuals from the sales. They initially made an offer to give Rockwilder $8000 upfront and a small percent of sales on the backend. I communicated this to Rockwilder, and he said he would take the deal. Outside of what we were already doing, it was the first transaction I negotiated on his behalf. It was a small deal, but nevertheless generated some positive income.

I told the ringtone company that he would do it for $10,000. They agreed and the following week, the check was in my hand. I had told Rockwilder what I was going to do so he could keep the entire $8000. He was all good with it.

Wisdom and Understanding Note

I learned, a long time ago, the initial offer is the low ball. It can never hurt to see if there is room for a reasonable increase in the first stage of a negotiation. Sometimes you can go way higher to work your way down to what you want. In this case, the company didn't even flinch at the extra $2000 and did the deal with no questions.

SELL MORE BEATS!

Just over a year and a half into running Rocbattle.com, we had over 5,000 producers and close to 40,000 members on the website. Many of the producers were doing well for themselves making an extra $500 to $2,000 every month from the website. It was a great thing that our website could provide such an opportunity. However, many of the producers started to get jealous because they couldn't sell as many beats, which they thought were better.

One day, while I was on the chat forums, I noticed a thread that complained about the top-selling producers. What was being said was that their beats were not all that good, yet they were at the top of the charts. I noticed that many music producers agreed about the producers at the top. Their main complaint was that their beats were better, so why were they not on the top of the charts? My only answer to them was they didn't know how to market.

Instead of replying in that forum, I had the idea to give them the information they needed in a course. As I have always done in the past, I looked for the problem, and then found a way to present the solution that would monetize. Just a few months before, my friend, Greg, had told me about a software called Camtasia Studios. This software would allow you to record your computer screen, which could then be used to create training videos. I decided to record a step-by-step training series for music producers to sell more beats. This course consisted of forty videos covering approximately ten hours of teaching. Once I recorded the first twenty-one videos, I put them in a secure area of my website (SellMoreBeats.com) and charged a membership access fee of $47.

Wisdom and Understanding Note

If you ever see individuals complaining about a problem, it may be an opportunity for you to introduce the solution. Money is spent to solve problems. Even when money is spent on

> entertainment, it solves the problem of boredom. The question is how you will train your mind to see problems you can fix.
> Your mindset should be, "There is always money in problems."

I went back to Rocbattle, where many of the music producers hang in the forum. I revealed in a new thread that if any producer was having a hard time selling his beats, I had a new site where they can learn how to sell more beats. I dropped the link to the new site, and within two weeks' time, I sold a thousand of those courses. The courses taught them how to market their beats, name their beats, create a website for their beats, optimize their website for the search engines --basically, everything a producer needed to market and sell beats. I wasn't sure exactly how many of these courses I would sell, so I was surprised that I sold 1,000 of them so fast and continued to sell another 1,000 over the next few months. All I did was monetize the information which was the solution to their problem. About a month later, I released another four hours of training and called it, "Advance Strategies to Sell More Beats." Over 50% of those who purchased the first course upgraded to purchase the advanced course.

Many of those producers tell me to this day, how helpful the course was. One of the producers sent me a letter telling me that the information helped him make $13,000 selling beats, while another made $700 the next week after taking my course. It had taken me one night to record twenty-one videos of the course, and a week to finish another twenty videos.

The sellmorebeats.com income was another result of the Million Dollar Seed. The idea to do a website came from a problem that music producers were having on Rocbattle.com

Sell More Beats Testimonials

Subj: Your Sellmorebeats Series has helped Me Tremendously!!!!!
Date: 11/19/2008 10:13:38 P.M. Eastern Standard Time
From: gl████████b.com
To: a████████████com

Allen, what's going on? This is R████████. I produce beats with my partner Q████████z. He is currently ranked #10 all-time on your site, RocBattle.com under the name (K████████). At the beginning of this year, I purchased your sellmorebeats series and it has helped us tremendously.

In 2005, I graduated college with a degree in Business Administration, but found it hard to find a quality job due to my past record stemming from events that happened when i was in high school. So I sought out to turn my hobby of making beats into a career. From 2005 to the beginning of 2008, all I did was make beats everyday along with Qz. We had hundred of beats stacked up and the industry exec and A&R's were giving us the run around. I knew we had to do something because we had too much good material just sitting inside our keyboards and computers. I know we had to put the same effort we use to make the beats into marketing the beats. I just wasn't sure how to attack it. That's when we came across SellMoreBeats.

To actually watch you build a website, and demonstrate how to generate traffic and income opened my eyes to new possibilities. Even when i was in college, no one showed me how to build a website step-by-step. Professors may have touched on the concept, but never a step-by-step tutorial. Plus the videos are much easier to understand and comprehend than reading it from a 300-page book. I built my own site with the information I learned from the videos. Once I applied some of your techniques to the site, i saw my traffic increase, along with sells. When i saw my sells increase, I knew I had to purchase the advance strategies. Those videos were just as good. We made close to $13,000 this year selling beats online. ████ and I are currently working on a new concept. We're going to hit you up on the One-on-One phone session on urban millionaire to get your opinion on the concept. You're like the Bill Gates of marketing beats on the Internet. Lol. I
definitely value your opinion. I got one question, what program did you use to setup your affiliate program for sellmorebeats.com? I really appreciate your time Allen.

Rick ████████████s
Rocbattle.com/K████████
IG████████

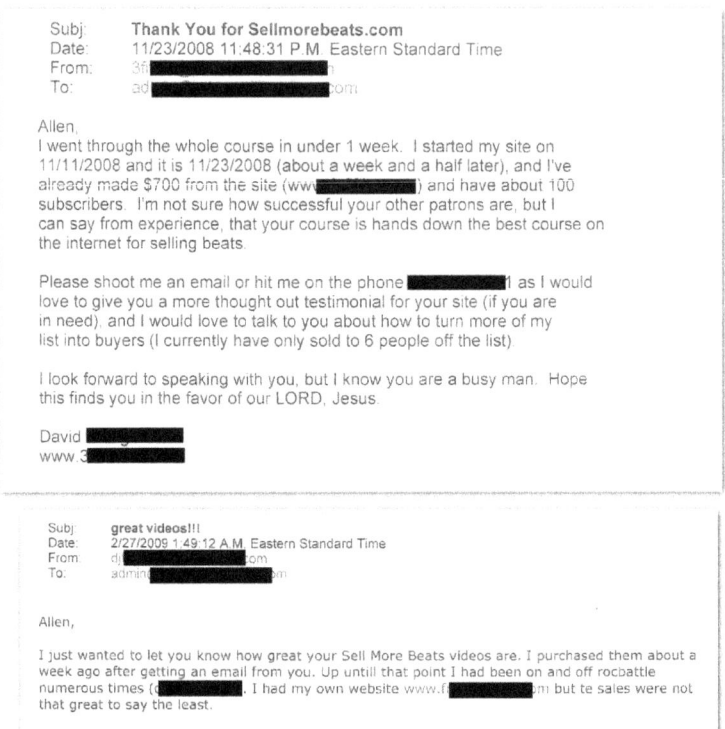

BEAT MACHINE SOFTWARE COMPANY

After Rocbattle.com had been up and running for a little over three years, Rockwilder came to me about a company in Tennessee. This company had a beat machine that they were trying to market but were failing at doing so. They saw that Rocbattle had a large following of music producers and was looking to do business. I reviewed their product and discovered what could be done for their marketing, so I agreed to meet with them. Once this company got word that we would help them, they flew us out to Tennessee to meet with all their executives and investors.

This was the first time a company had flown me out to meet with them. I was kind of nervous and excited at the same time. I knew what they needed and what I could help them with, so I was very confident. When we arrived at their office, I was able to meet not only the executives, but also the investors in the company. They began to share with me that they were owners of a half a billion-dollar real estate company, and they knew much about real estate. However, they expressed to me that they had invested in this electronic company and were losing money because they had no idea how to market it. I said, "That's the reason I'm here."

That same night, we went to dinner to discuss the issues and the possible direction for the company. After I evaluated everything, I told them I could get them out of debt with that company and get them started making sales with their beat machine. In the nine months before I got there, they had only sold 111 copies of their beat machine software. I assured them that those numbers were about to change.

After we completed the negotiations and I knew the percentages Rockwilder and I would make, they told me that we would have our deal complete within a few days. We flew back to New York and in a few days, we had completed the contracts. I told them to give me thirty days and a $1,000 budget, and I would put together a new website, a new marketing video, and a plan to execute. They agreed!

As soon as I started to work on this project, I started to get some resistance from the founders. They did not want me to make certain changes. They were currently selling the software for $150 each. I told them that we could sell over a million copies of the software if they reduced the price to $25. They could then sell the sound packs separately. They seemed to think that this would devalue their product. In all honesty, the product was not as valuable as they thought. There were other products in the market performing better than their product which could be purchased at lower prices. I was met with some other resistance, but I continued because I really was not in a position to force them to make the needed changes.

As I was coming up to the thirty-day mark, I needed one more week to make sure everything was in place. They seemed to get a little impatient but really had no choice. The following week came, and we were ready to go. I had put all the plans in place to sell their beat software at the price point they desired. I knew there would be some resistance in the market, but I continued anyway.

The first-month sales report came in, and they had sold almost $70,000 worth of software, which is just over 450 copies. This made them confident in the plans that I had executed with them. The main investor called me after the first month's report and said he was flying to New York to meet with me. We met at a Manhattan hotel restaurant and discussed further what could be done with the company. I began to share with him everything that I thought was hindering the company from being a success.

I told him that the founders he invested in were overpricing the product. I urged him to reduce the price to $25 instead of $150.

Even though we had sold over 450 copies, we could have sold 10,000 copies had they been priced at $25. He was reluctant, so I shared with him other things that could be changed within the company. He told me that the three founders were each making $3,000 per month. I asked him why the company was in the red and 1.5 million in debt. Why were the investors still allowing all three founders to draw salaries? I never fully understood the reason why they committed to paying them.

He went on to tell me that the company was spending close to $55,000 a month on operating costs. The investors were doing capital calls every month to keep things afloat. He said that he would take my suggestions to lower the monthly cost, but the founders' salary could not change. After some research, I got their monthly operating costs down to about $18,000 a month. Previously, they were paying a popular ad agency $18,000 each month for four consecutive months. I told him to fire that agency because they were not getting any results. In the last six months, they had only sold 111 copies. They didn't need the web developer who was being paid $4,000 per month but who was doing about $200 worth of work. I offered to do his job for free. The meeting in New York opened the budget for them to make more money and allowed them to pay me more money.

Within a few months' time, they asked me to be their COO (Chief Operating Officer) which entailed me flying to Tennessee twice a month to oversee operations. They paid me $5,000 a month on top of the sales commissions of each beat machine software I was selling. This arrangement made me just over $100,000 and allowed me to keep my freedom. I eventually stepped down from the COO position because they wanted me to do more that would take away time from my business. To me, that would have been an absolute "no go."

This opportunity was another illustration of how God honored His promise to bless me with the finances needed to have free time with my family. It was the result of the seed I had sown so long ago.

BEAT WEBSITE SOFTWARE

In January 2010, Rockwilder said he wanted to revamp the Rocbeats.com, and I told him I would start working on it right away. I had a lot of things going on, so I decided to outsource the project and hire some developers to do much of the web development. It took about three and a half months to complete and the new website was ready to go.

I contacted Rockwilder and let him know the new site was ready to go. He told me he wasn't sure if the solo site was what he wanted to do at the moment. I reminded him that I spent a lot of money to get it done. He said he understood, but he was just not up for the task right now. Now, I was stuck with a $3,300 website built from scratch, wondering what I could possibly do with it.

I would often register domains I thought sounded good and could possibly be great ideas. I had over 200 domain names at that time. When Rockwilder told me that he really didn't feel like doing the new website now, I started brainstorming. What am I going to do with this web script I just paid for? Then I thought *What if I make a beat website software that lets me sell the script as a cookie-cutter website for music producers?* I went to look over my domain names and saw that I had registered the name Beatwebsites.com a few months prior. That's when it all came to me. I could develop a software company that would allow music producers to have their own websites at very little expense.

The only thing I had to figure out was how to allow producers to purchase the software and protect it from being illegally copied. After I figured all those things out, I was ready to start marketing the beat software. I created a pre-sale campaign. This allowed me to raise $10,000 by selling 400 copies two months before the actual launch date. That turned out to be a good move because I covered the expenses of what I had paid for the development and all the needed upgrades before the launch date. The Beatwebsites.com software has grown to three different releases and generated over $175,000 in just over four years.

This is another result of the seed that was sown and why I call it the Million Dollar Seed. Even though this wasn't something Rockwilder and I worked on, it was still a blessing because of how it came about. If Rockwilder hadn't asked me to upgrade Rocbeats.com and then changed his mind, I may have never launched my beat website software. The Million Dollar Seed was still at work!

THE MILLION DOLLAR SEED NEVER STOPS

There were many other income opportunities that grew from the Million Dollar Seed. The countless knowledge gained from each venture is worth more than millions. Web consulting, marketing consulting, web development—even this book—can be linked to the Million Dollar Seed. I don't think you can put a value on such an act of faith.

When I share my story with some people, it's extremely hard for them to believe what God has done through my faith. I have to be honest with you. It's sometimes hard for me to believe. When I really think about it, it really didn't take that long. I sold everything in February 2003, and by December 2005, my business started taking off. The cultivation time in-between was less than a three-year period. How long are you willing to wait for God to bring your vision to pass?

EXACTLY WHAT I PRAYED FOR

When I first prayed to God, I had no idea what He would do for me. I just know that I was tired and wanted a serious change. When God answered me and told me what to do, I was hesitant. At times, I didn't move forward as quickly as I should have. However, I do believe God still timed everything for me perfectly. He promised to bless me and give me the financial freedom I desperately desired. God honored His Word, and He made good on His promises.

The most amazing part was that I was able to attend all my family events and never had to worry if I was losing any money. Unlike my days at the barbershop where I had limited time and freedom, the websites provided me more than enough time. These businesses allowed me to not only have Saturdays off but the entire week to do whatever I wanted to do. I became the coach for two of my sons' football teams and never had to worry about not being able to make it to a game. I would take family trips and extend our visits for however long we wanted to stay. I often joked with my wife, saying that we lived like retired folks in our thirties. This was all the result of us trusting God.

BACK TO MY FIRST LOVE

In January of 2017, I put together a course to help barbers learn how to grow a successful barber business since I had good success with it as an owner of two barbershops, from 1993 up until 2003, before I sold my " Short Cuts" barber shop to my friend, Dasul. The strangest thing happened when I finished producing the 5 hour video course. I missed cutting hair and had a strong desire to want to start cutting hair again.

I went to my wife and told her how I was feeling. "I thought you never wanted to cut hair again" was her reply. I told her that I never wanted to feel obligated and frustrated to cut hair ever again, and that there was a strong passion building up in me to open a barber shop. Within 30 days of that conversation, and 5 weeks after I completed the BarberShopCashFlow.com website, I was the owner of a new barber shop in my town. God did something amazing with this venture in setting it up. There was blessing after blessing that came after the shop opened. My second son, Isaiah, took a liking to cutting hair and became a licensed barber in the state of Pennsylvania and New York at the age of seventeen. God unleashed a series of blessings and directions that now has me as the owner of the very first Barber School in my city. The barbershop and the barber school are located right next door to each other. Something else that God did which I will discuss later. God is AMAZING, *Thank you JESUS!*

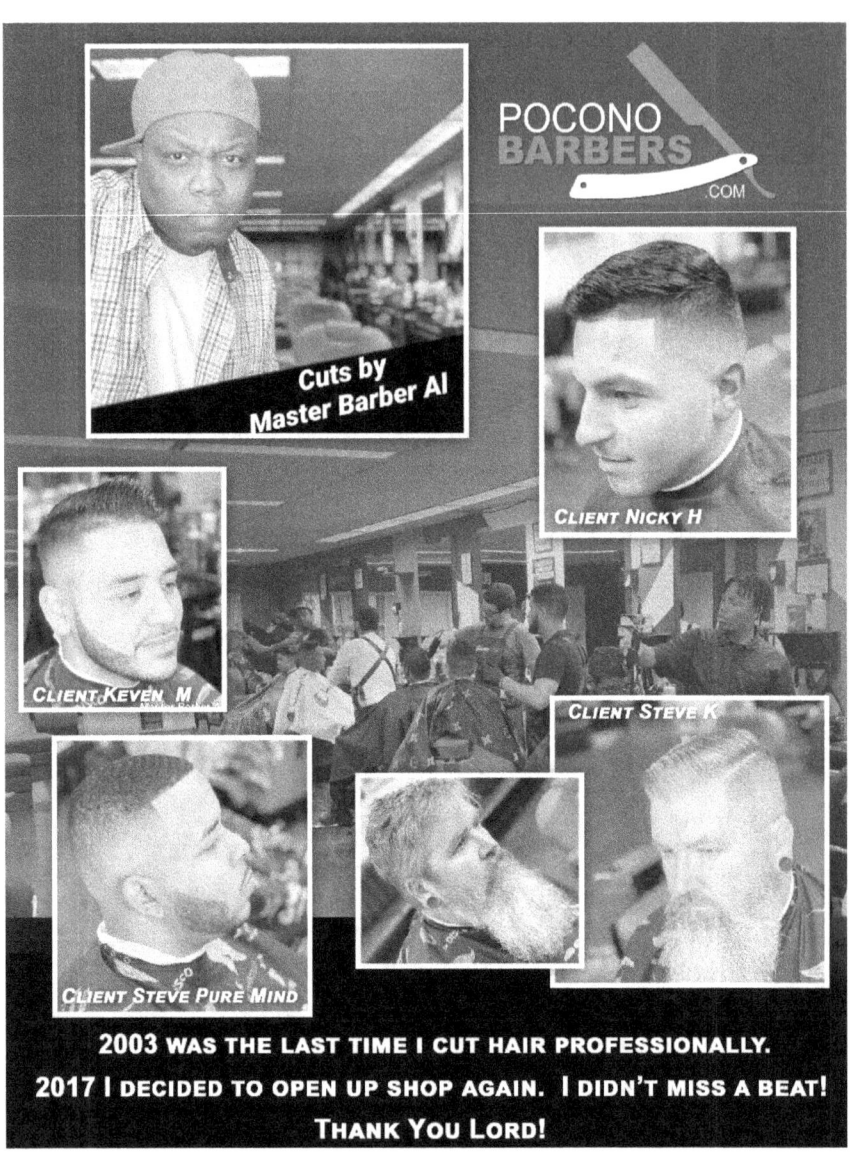

**2019 SUCCESS BARBER ACADEMY, LLC OPENED
TEACHING OTHERS THE CRAFT
THANK YOU LORD!**

CHAPTER 17

ONLY GOD KNEW!

I felt it necessary to share what I believe to be many of the behind-the-scenes things God did in my life. There are many dots in your life that God will connect. Pay close attention to them all because there are no such things as coincidences. I want you to know every person, place, or thing in your life is there for a reason. Having a perspective like that, your world can open, and you will see how God has always been on your side. Through the good and bad from before day one, He has been there. Something I like to say whenever it's revealed to me what God has done behind the scenes is, **"ONLY GOD KNEW!***"*

MY CHILDHOOD FUELED MY AMBITION

God couldn't have blessed me with better parents. I only knew love and protection my entire childhood. My parents instilled great morals in me which made me want to succeed and do things the right way. Some of my friends turned to sell drugs to get fast money. I'm 100% sure I could have gone that route, being in close proximity to people who could get me involved. However, I stayed away from it so I would never be in a position to disappoint my parents.

From 1989 through 1990, my parents had a rough patch in the real estate business. They both were real estate agents. My father had become a licensed real estate broker after his bus driver career came to an end due to injury. During that time, the real estate market crashed and for about a year, things were tight. My father pulled me to the side a few times to explain the finances. At age fourteen, I got my first understanding of real life.

I believe these conversations changed my life and added an extra drive for me to push beyond the norm. I also believe God exposes us to different ups and downs in our lives to fuel inspiration or give us drive. For me, the circumstances stopped me from asking my parents for money and gave me the drive to work hard for my own.

At fourteen years old, I picked up a pair of clippers and owned my own barbershop within five years. I didn't plan any of that; I just continued on the path that was before me.

ONLY GOD KNEW!

Only God knew I would step out to try a new opportunity and within a few months, own the barbershop. I sure had no clue that Opie would default on his lease agreement and leave it open for me to be blessed. ***Only God Knew!***

THE PERFECT WIFE FOR THE JOURNEY

A few weeks before I met my wife, I clearly stated I was not getting married, but within minutes of meeting her, I knew she would be my wife. How in the world did that happen?

About two years into our marriage, we were at a holiday gathering where several women were in attendance. Somehow the question was asked, "If your man was broke, would you live in a cardboard box with him?" All the women in the room gave their answers: capital "N-O." My wife was the last one in the circle. When it was her turn, she said, "Yes." Now, of course, it was funny to all the women in the room, but to me, it put a distinction on who God had given me as a wife.

Not only did she trust me with the decisions I had to make for the both of us and our children, but she also offered no major resistance for the vision God gave me and responded accordingly to help us move forward. This meant giving up a home, a business, and money. It also meant being uncomfortable living in a home that was not hers--all to support the vision. We didn't have to live in a cardboard box, but as far as I'm concerned, she proved she was a "ride or die woman" for me.

> **ONLY GOD KNEW!**
> At the time of this writing, it's been twenty-three years since I met my wife and twenty-two years since we married. God knew exactly what kind of woman I needed for the journey and for the process He would put me through. Not many spouses would agree with their partner giving away everything and then living with in-laws to start over.
>
> As I shared in chapter four, we had our ups and downs, but every challenge made us better and stronger. I know God connected us, but how He made her and shaped her mentally to be exactly what I needed is something beyond amazing to me. ***Only God Knew!***

GOD LIFTED THE WEIGHT SO I COULD FLY

The last thing I would expect God to do was instruct me to give all my money away. My logic, which is stupidity to God, could not see the wisdom in His request. I spent four years in my parents' house receiving wisdom from God that I would have not learned if I hadn't followed His instructions. I learned many things by submitting to His process.

The first thing that God showed me was that I was carrying too much weight. The home mortgage, car payment, business rent, bills, and other monthly expenses, put me in a position that kept me working just to pay the bills. God, in His wisdom, answered me in prayer to get rid of everything. Only God knew that, once everything was gone, I would be able to sit still for a period and work freely without worrying about paying bills. I was fully able to focus on all the new skill sets (graphic design, web development, sales, and marketing, etc.) while I was at my parents' home. This was something I couldn't do working every day. I had no energy left after work to pursue the new vision.

The second thing God showed me was I can trust him. Without submitting to the process, I never would have known that I could eat out of God's hand. When I was completely broke, God showed me that He could make money come from anywhere as long as I followed him. I hadn't known before then what it was like to wait on God for each meal. From a young age, I always worked and was able to provide for my family and myself. God showed me, in more ways than one, that I can trust Him when being led by His Spirit.

ONLY GOD KNEW!

Many people don't realize they have put themselves in a trap and can't get out because of the monthly obligations they created for themselves. I fully understand now why God had me give everything away. The benefit of being able to fully concentrate on what you really want for your life can all come to pass when you remove the things that are weighing you down. Who knew that if I got rid of all my stuff and humbled myself, I could focus on the things I really wanted and prayed for, and receive them. ***Only God Knew!***

THE LOVE FOR MUSIC

For as long as I can remember, I have loved music. When I was in middle school, the entire fifth and sixth-grade classes were called to an assembly to see who was musically inclined. The music teacher called the children up to the piano. She would play the piano to see who could follow the tones. I remember repeating every sound she played and her saying that I did extremely well mimicking her. The next thing I knew, I was enrolled in music class and asked what instrument I wanted to play. I decided to play the trumpet and played it until the tenth grade when I switched to the baritone horn.

In high school, I finished four semesters of music theory to graduate with a music theory diploma. Once I left high school, I wasn't sure if I would continue to pursue anything that involved music. That all changed in 1994 when I went to visit my friend, Jonathan's house. He had a studio in his basement, and that visit totally inspired me to build a studio and get back into music.

I made a little money and even sold a few beats in my early twenties. My music and my production company didn't take off, but I learned a lot in that time. When I met my wife in 1997, I decided to put music down and ended up selling or donating all the equipment I had.

ONLY GOD KNEW!

Only God knew I would go to a school that would offer a music program. This program would help me enhance my skills in music and lend support to all my music endeavors. Who knew that, in 2004, He would connect me with one of the biggest music producers in the industry to start a website that generated millions of dollars? ***Only God Knew!***

ROCKWILDER BEFORE I PERSONALLY KNEW HIM

I knew Rockwilder as a music producer before our divine connection. I can remember exactly where I was when I heard two of his beats, in particular. I was in my barbershop when a car stopped in front. It had a nice loud system, and it was blasting music. The barbershop door was opened, and I could hear the song playing in the shop. What caught my ear was the intro of the production. As a music producer, my mouth dropped. "What in the world?" is something I often say when I'm blown away. The name of the song was called "Da Rockwilder" and was performed by the rappers, Redman, and Method Man. The song was less than three minutes long and changed the sound of hip hop production at that time. As a music producer, I took note of the production and discovered exactly who he was.

I heard the second beat from him when I went to visit my friend, Damian, at his barbershop. He let me hear a song where he rapped over a Jay-Z beat. I had stopped following hip hop at the time, so I didn't know it was a beat that Jay-Z had come out with originally. After he played the song for me, I said, "That beat is crazy!" Come to find out the original song was called "Do It Again."

What made both productions so amazing is that Rockwilder created beat intros never heard in hip hop. His beat production, in general, broke the mold of traditional hip hop music productions. He broke the rules with the Jay-Z beat by doing a three-bar beat. It was an amazingly unique beat style.

> **ONLY GOD KNEW!**
> As I took note of this new hip hop production style, I sought out the producer. It was then I discovered who Rockwilder was. Little did I know that, in a few years, God would link us together to create a music production website and help beatmakers from all around the world sell their music. ***Only God Knew!***

SO FAR AWAY BUT YET SO CLOSE

My good friend, Greg, who I had grown up with, was very instrumental in many of the things I was exposed to. In 1994, he was the one who gave me the book, *Think and Grow Rich* by Napoleon Hill. He had known Rockwilder personally years before I did. They used to hang out with each other, but he didn't know him as Rockwilder but by his real name, Dana Stinson. When I told him I had connected with the music producer, Rockwilder, he didn't know who I was talking about. Then, when I showed Greg a picture of him, he told me they used to hang out together.

The reason I'm sharing this with you is because I started to discover many people I knew also knew Rockwilder personally. I was always one person away from Rockwilder for years, but it wasn't until God said it was time for us to meet that we connected. I guess no one was going to get the glory for the connection but God!

ONLY GOD KNEW!

Once I started to discover how close Rockwilder and I were as far as people and location were concerned, I knew God had His hand on the timing. We lived in the same community--only four or five blocks from each other. We had close friends we had both known for years. This is a big deal to me because when God led me to his mother's church to sow the financial seed, I probably would have talked myself out of it. I think my flesh would have questioned God to justify why that church needed my support. I'm glad God kept me blind and set it up exactly how He did. ***Only God Knew!***

TWO MILLION PLUS RECORDS SOLD

I was blessed to meet Fat Joe and the new artist, Big Pun, in the studio while I was working on music production for an independent artist. The album Fat Joe was working on was for Big Pun's Debut Album *Capital Punishment*. I'm not sure how life would have been if I had made that album, but I do know that God's plan for us is way better than what we think is good for us.

What I didn't know until I met Rockwilder was that he had two of the biggest songs on that album: "Super Lyrical" (featuring Black Thought) and "You Came Up" (featuring Noreaga). The album consisted of twenty-four songs. When I met Rockwilder and told him about the meeting I had in the studio, he shared some wisdom with me. He told me that since Fat Joe and Big Pun liked the beat that got me the meeting, I should have given the $500 back to the artist that purchased it and told him that I wanted Big Pun to have it. Now I'm not 100% sure I would have done that, but knowing these types of things can happen, it would have been smart for me to put that in the contracts beforehand. In other words, if said artist does not release the music in a certain amount of time, I would then be able to sell it to someone else.

ONLY GOD KNEW!

It was fifteen years later when Rockwilder shared that knowledge with me. Looking at it now, I believe things worked out the way they were supposed to. It may have made the course of my life a little different if we had known each other from that point on and been on the same album. Sometimes I wonder how it would have been to have a song on an album that sold more than two million copies. However, I'm extremely grateful God did it His way. Only God Knew!

ROTTWEILER DREAM

The Sunday before I went to sow the seed at Rockwilder's mother's church, I had a dream. If you remember, the dream was so real that I woke up in a sweat. I even looked out the window to see if there were dogs in my neighbor's yard. Dreams that feel so real are the ones I never forget.

ONLY GOD KNEW!

When I met Rockwilder, he told me a story of how he obtained his name. He was walking down the street with a group of friends and had his sweat hood over his head. One of the young ladies turned to him and said that he looked like a rottweiler dog with the way he had the hood over his head. He was a music producer at the time and thought it would be perfect to call himself "Rockwilder" instead of Rottweiler. I can't think of any other reason why I had that dream but to give me confirmation of the connection I was going to make. I can't be 100% sure. ***Only God Knew!***

PUT MUSIC ON THE LEGAL HUSTING CDS

When I came up with the idea for the Legal Hustling CD's, I had no intention of adding hip hop music to them. I set the studio session up for three hours and went in to do the recording. I was only able to get about three-fourths of the recording down before my time was up. So, I had to come in the following day to complete the rest.

When I arrived at the studio the next day, the engineer shared an idea for the project. He had added hip hop music under my voice. It sounded good, and we finished it out with music throughout the entire recording.

ONLY GOD KNEW!

When I met Rockwilder's mother, she asked me what I did for a living. I told her that I did motivational speaking and teaching over hip-hop beats. Her reply was, "My son does hip hop beats." Although I believe God can make the connection any kind of way, there could have had an alternative ending if I would have booked in another music studio.

Another Possible Scenario

What if the engineer at the studio hadn't added the hip hop beats to my audio? I wouldn't have been able to give her the response I did, giving her no reason to mention Rockwilder. Sometimes I wonder how it would be if Rockwilder's name would not have come up. ***Only God Knew!***

AUNT NELL AND MY FIRST CLIPPER

I'm forever grateful that Aunt Nell gave me my first professional clipper. As I was putting this book together, I thought that I would tell her what it meant to me. I was going to wait until it was all finished and published to surprise her with a copy. However, on April 19, 2020, the Holy Spirit nudged me to get in contact with her now. I had not spoken to Aunt Nell for about a year and four months since her husband, Uncle David, had passed. I needed her number, so I reached out to my cousin, Kym, her daughter, for her cell phone number. The following day, I gave her a call.

She was extremely happy to hear from me. I thanked her for the clippers, and we laughed about it. I told her that she was in my new book, and she was happy to hear that. My wife and I spoke with her for a while, and we said our goodbyes. I was extremely happy I shared that with her.

> **ONLY GOD KNEW!**
> On April 23rd, four days after that call with Aunt Nell, I received a call from my mother telling me that Kym had called and said that Aunt Nell was home and unresponsive. I hung up the phone and immediately started praying. Midway through my prayer, I was having a hard time continuing, but I didn't stop. My mother called me back and said that Aunt Nell had passed away.
>
> My plan had been to give Aunt Nell a copy of this book when it was completed, but God spoke to me when I was putting her name in the dedication to get in contact with her now. You may never know why the Holy Spirit will prompt you to do something. The furthest thing from my mind then was that I would not see or hear from her again on this side of heaven. ***Only God Knew!***
>
> RIP Aunt Nell! I Love You!

When I started this chapter, I had no idea that the Lord would speak to my heart about a series of books I would soon be releasing. Each time I wrote 'Only God Knew,' it was being more and more embedded in my mind. In January of 2020, I was sitting at Olive Garden with a longtime friend, Deon, and he said I would soon be releasing more books every month. I thought to myself that I don't even write that fast. However, I didn't dismiss the thought.

In the first week of April 2020, I was on the phone with Rockwilder and he thought he heard me saying I would be releasing books. I replied and said, "No," only a book. After I went to correct him, I thought about what Deon said in Olive Garden a few months ago. My question to the Lord again was, *How? When I don't even type that fast.*

On April 12, 2020, I was in my kitchen thinking about another idea and just like that, I said, "Build Our Kingdom." Based on my thought for another possible venture, I went to Godaddy to see if that domain was available. I always get the domains for ideas that come to my head. So, BuildOurKingdom.com was available and I purchased the domain name.

On April 27, I was reviewing this book (Million Dollar Seed) and going over the Only God Knew chapter; God spoke to me, and said to make that my next book title. Without hesitation, I did the normal routine and registered OnlyGodKnew.com. Now I know I have many great stories and miracles to share about the goodness of God, but I needed to seek the Lord further to get clarity. As I laid in my bed, open to receive, God showed me the following vision:

God showed me that I would soon be releasing a full series of anthology books with various authors, testifying of His goodness with true life testimonies and miracles. I could not believe how fast that vision unfolded. The crazy part was when I asked the Lord the direction to publish the series, He brought to memory the domain name I had just registered on April 12, a few days back, *BuildOurKing.com*. I had forgotten the name and had to go to my account to confirm the domain, which all I remembered was that it had the word kingdom in it. This is how you now have 'Build Our

Kingdom Publishing' with the Million Dollar Seed being the first release. *God is Amazing!*

(Side Note - if you are a Christian author with a testimony and would like a promotion for your writings, contact me today!)

ALL THINGS WORK TOGETHER

I think it's amazing how God oversees your entire life to get you exactly where you need to be. From when you are born to who you are born to, as well as the experiences you have throughout your life, whether good or bad. Everything plays a part in getting you to a place where God wants you to be. There is nothing in your life that will not be used to get you to your expected end. Everything in your life means something. The key is, once you understand this point, you need to start asking God to reveal things to you so everything you went through, and currently going through, will start to make sense.

"And we know that all things work together for good to those who love God, to those who are the called according to *His* purpose." Romans 8:28 NKJV

CHAPTER 18

TELL THE WORLD

God gave me *The Million Dollar Seed* title in June 2010. I know the exact date because I always registered domain names based on the ideas I had. The same day it came to my mind, I went to godaddy.com and purchased the MillionDollarSeed.com. Again, the reason I have so many domain names. When I get ideas, I go to see if anyone has taken the domain name so I can possibly market the idea online in the future. *(Side Note: You can always visit whois.net or other domain history websites to find original creation dates of domains.)*

I had all intentions to start writing this book, but I didn't think I would wait until January 2020, ten years later. Many things have happened in the past ten years, but the events of the last few months of 2019 pushed to get this book out now.

The number of people that knew my testimony had been minimal. Before the writing of this book, I shared my testimony a few times in a few churches where I was speaking. I also shared it briefly in my Sell More Beats online course in 2008. Besides that, a few other people that I met knew my story. I knew that one day, God would have me get to it, but it wasn't until November 2019 that I started to get direct signals from the Lord to move forward with sharing my story with the world.

THE LAST MESSAGE FROM ARCHBISHOP LESTER WILLIAMS

I was on my way back from a meeting in New York on November 7, 2019, when my wife sent me a text that our first pastor, now Archbishop, Lester Williams had died. I could not believe what I read and called her immediately. She told me that someone else we knew at the church posted it on their Facebook timeline. I was in complete shock for the remainder of my ride back home to Pennsylvania.

I know from all my years walking with God that there is no such thing as a coincidence. Just days before I heard the news of Archbishop Williams' passing, an email he sent me earlier popped up while I was searching for something else. I am not sure of the date, but I do know for a fact it was less than seven days prior to me learning his passing that this email popped up on my screen. I thought about reaching out to him, but for some reason or another, I didn't. In the email, he shared what a lady who attended his church luncheon had told him after I shared my testimony with the group. I was one of the speakers at the luncheon and had shared my testimony with those in attendance. She had been about to leave but decided to stay to hear me speak. She told him that my story was a blessing to her life and that she was overwhelmed by it. Further in the email, he stated that he would live the rest of his life-giving all he could for the Kingdom's sake and that he would die empty. This email was dated November 7, 2009-- exactly ten years to the date that I got the news that he had passed away.

Email From Bishop Williams
November 7, 2009

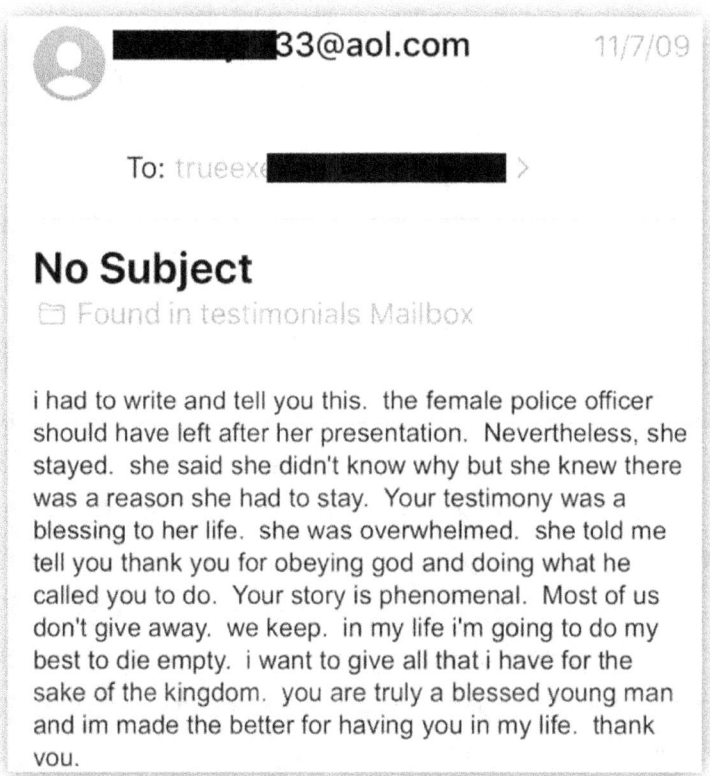

The next few days were strange to me. When someone close to you dies, it's kind of a weird feeling. Just to know that you will not see them anymore in this world. A few days later, as I was lying in bed thinking about him. I decided to pick up my phone to look on social media. As soon as I put my access code in, the phone opened to the next screen. There again, was the email he had written to me. Strange! When it popped up the first time before I knew that he had died, I was on my office computer. This time, it popped up on my phone, and I hadn't accessed my email account from the phone. I dismissed it, thinking that maybe I had somehow done it but forgotten. This time, I made sure to clear my email, close the email app, and make a mental note of doing so.

Days after Archbishop Williams' funeral, I had been using my phone frequently, at least a dozen times or so. One day, I was thinking about him when I went to access my phone, and his email to me was once again right there on my screen! This time, I was overwhelmed and thought for sure there was a message I needed from this.

As I studied the email, it started to speak to me in many ways. One thing that kept coming out of it to me was the fact that the woman's life had been changed, as was his from hearing my testimony. This set in my spirit to start sharing my testimony again.

The following Sunday, I went to one of the local churches where I had fellowshipped with my family a few times, Family of God Church, Inc., pastored by Bishop Derek Pittman. When I walked in the church, a lady mistook me for a preacher she knew from New Jersey. I assured her that I wasn't him, and started to walk away. She stopped me and told me that I had a Word in me. I thought, *Why did she say that?* The reason was made evident shortly after.

Bishop Pittman knew that I had just opened a barber school in our community and had previously asked me to come to his church to announce it. On this day, I had no intention of speaking about the new barber school; I just wanted to come and worship the Lord with his church. Plans changed, though, when Bishop Pittman insisted that I come up and speak.

I prepared myself to share what God had done for me in opening a barber school. My testimony ended up being squeezed in so that the events made sense to everyone. At the end of the service, many of the congregants were extremely touched by the entire testimony. The lady who had mistaken me for a minister she thought she knew came over and said, "I told you, you had a word."

God began to lead me to visit different churches, in my area, of pastors that I had grown to know over the years in Pennsylvania. Some visits were my first time and others, my second or third. On the last Sunday in 2019, I visited Pastor Betty Grant's church, Mountaintop Christian Community Church. I had known her for about ten years, but I had never gone to her church. That Sunday morning, God led me there.

Once in the service, she did something that she never does. Right before she was ready to preach, she said she felt the Lord tell her that someone had a testimony. At that moment, one of the elders in the church started to walk towards me with the microphone. I just looked at her as she was walking towards me, thinking, I *didn't ask for that microphone.* She handed it to me anyway. I began to share my testimony about how I happened to open a barber school when I didn't have all the requirements to do so, along with how God had made all the connections for it to happen. The pastor then shared with the church that God had told her that He had a testimony that needed to be heard. Once I finished speaking, the service proceeded.

After the service, Pastor Grant and I were talking, and I started sharing everything that happened to me over the last fifteen years. She said, "No matter what you do or where you go, you have to tell your testimony to the world. Every chance you get going forward in the new year, tell your testimony. If you go to a church, and they call you out, share that testimony." That stuck with me. From that Sunday until January 1, 2020, I kept playing it over and over in my head.

On New Year's Day, I was sitting in my office, thinking about Archbishops Williams' email, Pastor Grant's words to me, and the few church services where I had recently shared my testimony. In that moment, God brought back to remembrance the domain name I had secured ten years previously with the intention of sharing my testimony: MillionDollarSeed.com. Without delay, I started writing the outline for this book and within four months, it was completed.

GOD'S TIMING IS PERFECT

I felt like God had me wait ten years to put my testimony in a book because of the many things that came after 2010. On top of that, the timing was perfect for me to share the story of what God has done in my life. I believe the people of God need to hear about true acts of faith where God blessed greatly because of obedience.

When I prayed to God and asked him to give me time with my family, I didn't know how He would do it. I do know that I believed He *could* do it. Like Abraham, I had to do my part and start the journey. Believe in God today and have total faith that He will show you the way.

"In all your ways acknowledge Him, And He shall direct your paths." Proverbs 3:6

MY PRAYER FOR YOU

It is my prayer for you that as you have read this book, your faith increases. That you see how following and accepting the Lord Jesus Christ changed my life. I believe God wants everyone to be blessed. He simply wants you to follow him so He can make your life what He has designed it to be.

It starts with accepting him in your heart and allowing Him to be your Lord. He already knows all about you; the Good and the

Bad. Don't make the mistake and wait until you think you are perfect enough to seek Him. Seek Him now so He can make you over now! In the Bible, Jesus spoke on more than ten occasions to "Follow me." It's in our following Him that many promises come for us to be blessed and made over by the Lord. Will you trust Him today!

YOUR SALVATION

The Bible says, "Jesus answered and said to him, "Most assuredly, I say to you, unless one is born again, he cannot see the kingdom of God." John 3:3 NKJV. The process starts with you being Born Again of his Spirit. It is then that you can enter the kingdom of God and obtain your salvation through the Lord Jesus Christ. "If you declare with your mouth, "Jesus is Lord," and believe in your heart that God raised him from the dead, you will be saved." Romans 10:9 NIV

My story testifies to the glory of God, and you can see what God can do when you believe totally in him to make a way for you. God is waiting for those who will step out and trust HIM, and believe Him at His Word. If you never trusted God totally with all your heart, do it *NOW* and accept Jesus in your heart, starting today!

CONCLUSION

UNDERSTANDING THE SEED

Since my book is titled *Million Dollar Seed,* I felt the need to conclude and explain a little about the seed as a powerful biblical principle. Many people overlook the seed principle but doing so can hold you in a place where you will never receive God's unthinkable blessings. It's my belief that once you read this book, you will have a new perspective on what God can do in your own life.

"Seeds" shape your entire life. There are seeds of exposure which penetrate your mind to provoke actions. Then from your actions, you give birth to your own reality. All the actions you take could be considered the sowing process. The reality in which you live right now is the harvest produced from your actions (Sowing).

Many people unknowingly take actions that produce good and bad results. The worst thing is getting results in your life (Your Harvest) and not knowing how you got them. To get more understanding, we must investigate the Word of God to evaluate the process.

HOW SEED WORKS IN THE EARTH

The Bible makes multiple references to the seed. In the book of Genesis, one especially important principle of God is introduced. **"While the earth remains, Seedtime and harvest, Cold and heat, Winter and summer, And day and night Shall not cease" Genesis 8:22 NKJV.** God shows us that He set things in motion that will continue to be as long as the earth is in existence. When it comes to the earth's seasons, we are simply at the mercy of wherever we are geographically. However, when it comes to God's principle of seedtime and harvest, we are fully engaged in it whether we know it or not. Seedtime and harvest have a direct connection as to 1) how we came into existence, 2) the fruit that we bear, and 3) how we sow to receive blessings from God. Our life is wrapped up in this principle (Law set by God) manifesting in the following three different ways.

HOW WE COME INTO EXISTENCE

When God released your spirit into the earth realm, you made your way here through seedtime and harvest. It should be obvious how God did that for you. He sent you wrapped in a seed where the characteristics, traits, physical features, and every other descriptive distinction became you. We see first-hand, by observing our own growth, how God used seedtime and harvest for human existence.

As the seed that is planted in your mother's womb, He has a harvest assigned to your life. Scripture makes it abundantly evident that He has a plan for you and it starts from a seed **"For I know the plans I have for you," declares the Lord, "plans to prosper you and not to harm you, plans to give you hope and a future. 12 Then you will call on me and come and pray to me, and I will**

listen to you. 13 You will seek me and find me when you seek me with all your heart." Jeremiah 29:11-13 NIV). God knows the plans for you, so He is expecting you to be His harvest.

WHICH SEED DID YOU KEEP?

Another manifestation of seed is a word. Words spoken to you have power to change your life. On the contrary, they can also destroy your life. The words you allow to take root in your mind will be the one you operate from.

In Luke 8:11, The Parable of the Sower, Jesus shows us that the Word of God is seed. **"Now the parable is this: The seed is the word of God." Luke 8:11.** The master Teacher wanted to bring clarity to the kingdom of God and used parables to simplify His message for His listener. In this case, He likens the Word of God to a seed and says whoever keeps his Word (seed) would bear fruit. **"But the ones that fell on the good ground are those who, having heard the word with a noble and good heart, keep it and bear fruit with patience." Luke 8:15 NKJV.**

The parable breaks down four levels of individuals who all hear the Word of God (seed) and who all respond in different ways. However, it's only the hearer of the word that keeps the seed (Word) and can bear fruit. This is the first level of thought conception that many people miss, but you really must get it if you are going to bear good fruit.

Your life has been a series of actions that you have taken, based on a word that you allowed to be planted in you. It could be God's Word, the devil's word, a friend's word, or any word, but once you receive it ("Keep it" as Jesus says about His Word), you get the results of that word. The sum total of your life is based on the words (seeds) you have allowed to shape you. Hopefully, this makes it clear to you that God's principle of seedtime and harvest (Genesis 8:22) is working in your life, currently producing results from a word (seed) you allowed to impregnate your mind at some point.

THE SEED YOU SOW

Just like the word (seed) that is received by what we hear and see, there is the seed that you possess to get exactly what you need by sowing. God is not a liar, so when He says through the apostle Paul, **"Do not be deceived, God is not mocked; for whatever a man sows, that he will also reap," Galatians 6:7,** He meant every single word of it because it's a fixed law in the earth. "Whatever" in this scripture could mean anything, positive or negative; it will come back to you!

The seed you sow could be respect, honor, hospitality, money, love, etc., but understand that whatever you sow, and how you sow it, determines your harvest. For many people, this is an easy principle to understand, yet when it comes to applying it, many fail to follow through.

God is constantly providing you with seed, and it's your responsibility to sow. **"Now he who supplies seed to the sower and bread for food will also supply and increase your store of seed and will enlarge the harvest of your righteousness." 2 Corinthians 9:10 NIV,** "**Remember this: Whoever sows sparingly will also reap sparingly, and whoever sows generously will also reap generously." 2 Corinthians 9:6 NIV.** In all your giving, God wants you to do it big for a reason. To sow a seed sparingly simply means you have more to sow, but you restrict yourself. Could this mean that you don't trust the Lord?

The consciousness of you operating in all three will get you results beyond your belief. I know that is what happened to me when I look at the actions I took, what God put in me from the beginning of time, and how I think.

GOD DOESN'T HAVE FAVORITES

The Bible says that God is not a respecter of persons. **"For there is no partiality with God." Romans 2:11 NKJV**. God doesn't show favoritism, and since God does not show favoritism, a big part of getting anything extraordinary from God is first knowing that He doesn't break His principles. This means that whoever applies those principles to their life will reap the benefit of the principle being used. We don't all start in the same place in life, but we can all take hold and apply God's principles and get great results in the process of discovering what we were put here on earth to do.

THE MILLION DOLLAR SEED IN YOU

Now, you have all of the facts. The seed is powerful and it's a spiritual law placed here by God for you to be blessed and prosper. Never be limited to think you need money. You can start building a successful life by simply giving your time. Many people will sit in front of a television or remain on social media all day and wonder why there is no production (Forward movement) in their life. They are reaping what they sow. What you can do instead, is find a local business owner, or someone accomplished in what you want to do in life and start offering them your help for free. Start looking for opportunities where you can start to add value to someone's life or business. What you will be doing is sowing seed that will come back to you greatly.

Helping a successful business owner will allow you to be exposed to how to be successful. They may have never hired you, but because you came to offer value first without seeking money, you were connected and now, can be exposed to what you would have to do to obtain the same. Everything is not about a paycheck or how much you can get paid for an hour's worth of work, which is very limited in itself. Everything should be more about the harvest you can produce from the seeds you sow. Allow your mind to be transformed and seek the Lord for Godly principles, not the ones that the world has sold many people on. **"Do not conform to the pattern of this world, but be transformed by the renewing of your mind. Then you will be able to test and approve what God's will is— his good, pleasing and perfect will." Romans 12:2 NIV**

There is no excuse for you not to start following the Lord and giving Him all you got. I know we all fall short to God's glory. However, while there is still time to find him, you need to pursue Him with all your heart. You will be surprised what He has placed in you that can come out to be a blessing to yourself and others. But, you will never know unless you trust Him. Trust Him *TODAY*!

Message from The Author's Wife

It is often asked of me; how did I feel when my husband gave all our money away? I would be lying if I said it was easy. At times, I did get frustrated through the process. However, I trusted and believed in God, and in my husband.

I know what kind of man I married. My husband loves God and his family; he is a provider and is very family oriented. However, he did not just want to be a provider, he wanted to also be present in his family's lives.

For the fact that he is hard working, self-sufficient, and a go getter, I believe the process was harder for him than it was for me. Knowing he had no money and could have gone out to make money at any time, he instead chose to look silly by trusting and waiting on God's promise.

This taught me an incredible amount of faith, by watching him wait on God's promise.

I did not always agree with everything, but he considered my feelings through it all.

~ Melissa Brown ~

About the Author

Allen Brown is a successful entrepreneur who has helped many people achieve success by providing unique wisdom and insight to help change their life.

Allen owned his first business at the age of eighteen. This allowed him to obtain several more businesses early on, so much that he started earning a six-figure income by the age of twenty-two.

He met his wife at twenty-two and shortly after, became a born-again Christian. Five years after becoming a Christian, he found himself frustrated and struggling with not having enough time to spend with his family. He prayed about it and received a shocking answer. The only way the Lord was going to turn things around for Allen was through total trust in Him.

After submitting to God's process, doors began to open for Allen. He started generating millions of dollars, and he began to get all the free time he needed to enjoy his family. God blessed him with successful internet businesses and several other opportunities that provided the income and leverage he prayed for.

Allen passionately believes that the world needs to know that God is real, and God can do more for people than they can do for themselves. He uses his life and success in business as a practical example.

He attributes all of his success today to God's leading and inspiration, especially at times when things seemed difficult and impossible. Allen has dedicated his life to fully serving God as he currently pastors in Pennsylvania. Having tasted the practicality of God's Word and purpose, Allen describes himself as a teacher of the gospel of Jesus Christ with a focus on trusting God and using Godly principles to obtain the promises of God.

Above all, he spreads the goodness of the Lord Jesus Christ and teaches believers how to build their finances and economy by using Godly wisdom and principles.

When Allen isn't pastoring, or engaged in other activities, you'll find him with his beautiful wife of 23 years and their four sons.

The Million Dollar Seed is the first book published by Pastor Allen Brown.

About Build Our Kingdom Publishing

BUILD OUR KINGDOM PUBLISHING
BUILD OUR KINGDOM.COM

WE ARE A CHRISTIAN BOOK PUBLISHER WITH THE FOCUS ON PUBLISHING NON-FICTION LITERATURE TO EDIFY AND BUILD THE KINGDOM OF GOD.

OUR VISION IS TO SEE PEOPLE COME TO JESUS CHRIST AS A RESULT OF THE TITLES WE RELEASE.

 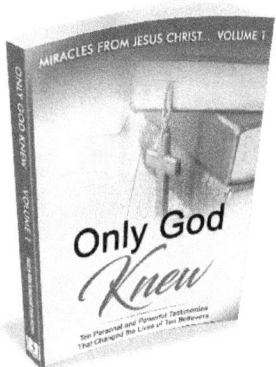

    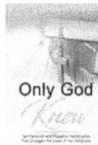  

Sow a Seed!

Remember this: Whoever sows sparingly will also reap sparingly, and whoever sows generously will also reap generously.
2 Corinthians 9:6

If the Million Dollar Seed book has been a blessing to you, please sow a seed to help spread the message.

Cash App $MillionDollarSeed

PayPal   paypal.me/milliondollarseed

By Mail:
Christian Believers Church, Inc.
PO Box 1079
Stroudsburg PA 18360

Your Financial Seed Helps To Spread the Goodness of Jesus Christ Around The World!

To contact the author:

Pastor Allen Brown

Christian Believers Church, Inc.

PO Box 1079

Stroudsburg PA 18360

For All Inquiries

Email: MillionDollarSeed@gmail.com

ChristainBelieversChurch.org

MillionDollarSeed.com

BuildOurKingdom.com

OnlyGodKnew.com

BarberShopCashFlow.com

SuccessBarberAcademy.com

PoconoBarbers.com

RocBattle.com

Beatwebsites.com

BuyBeats.com

DibThis.com

www.ingramcontent.com/pod-product-compliance
Lightning Source LLC
Chambersburg PA
CBHW071233080526
44587CB00013BA/1591